THE REFERENCE SHELF *(Continued)*

Volume 28

No.

1. Immigration and the United States. Poyntz Tyler. $2.

2. Juvenile Delinquency. G. S. McClellan. $2.

4. Community Planning. H. L. Marx, Jr. $2.

5. The Government and the Farmer. W. M. Daniels. $2.

6. The Middle East in the Cold War. G. S. McClellan. $2.

Volume 26

No.

5. The Censorship of Books. 2d printing. W. M. Daniels. $2.

Volume 24

No.

3. Representative American Speeches: 1951-1952. A. C. Baird. $1.75.

Volume 23

No.

2. Representative American Speeches: 1950-1951. A. C. Baird. $1.75.

Volume 22

No.

3. Representative American Speeches: 1949-1950. A. C. Baird. $1.75.

Volume 20

No.

5. Federal World Government. J. E. Johnsen. $1.50.

THE REFERENCE SHELF

Vol. 32 No. 2

THE NEW NATIONS OF WEST AFRICA

Edited by

ROBERT THEOBALD

THE H. W. WILSON COMPANY
NEW YORK 1960

Printed in the United States of America

Library of Congress Catalog Card No. 60-8240

PREFACE

The United States has never had a positive, dynamic policy for Africa. Until very recently, we have looked to the continuing control by friendly European powers as a guarantee of stability and dependable cooperation and have been reluctant to acknowledge the principle of self-government as fully applicable to its peoples. Yet in 1960 we shall be dealing with nine to ten fully independent states in sub-Saharan Africa alone, and a decade later with more than twice that number.[1]

The recognition of the validity of this statement has led to a considerable development of interest in Africa in the last few years. It has also resulted in a multitude of articles whose typical titles would be "Emerging Africa," "Awakening Africa," "Africa Out of Her Shell." In this book, an attempt is made to get below the surface, to probe the differences and similarities of the various countries discussed, to point out that Africa's problems are uniquely her own and not merely an extension of America's; and that they cannot therefore be solved by merely transferring American policies and ideas.

The scope of the book is described by its title, THE NEW NATIONS OF WEST AFRICA. Geographically, we are concerned with over twenty lands. Some of them are independent already; one of them, Liberia, has been independent for over a century. At least four additional countries in this part of Africa, the French Cameroons, French Togoland, the Belgian Congo, and Nigeria will attain independence in 1960, while some of the territories that were previously controlled by the French are also expected to achieve independence in the same year—although some form of association with France may well continue.

It is probably impossible to gain an adequate impression of the variety of these territories without a list of their size, population, and population densities. Such a list is given on

[1] *United States Foreign Policy: Africa; a Study,* prepared at the request of the Senate Committee on Foreign Relations by Northwestern University. Program of African Studies. United States. Senate. Committee on Foreign Relations. 86th Congress, 1st session. Supt. of Docs. Washington 25, D.C. '59. p 1.

page 11 below. It will be helpful to look at the map on the facing page while comparing these figures.

The vast differences in size of countries, population, and population density make it clear that the problems in the various countries will differ. In view of the variety of climate, from lush tropical jungle to desert; of language, each tribe with its own dialect and with English, French, Portuguese or Spanish superimposed by the colonizing power; and of access to raw materials, adequate transport facilities and power, separate examination of different areas is clearly required.

For this reason about half of this book, taken up by Section II, is devoted to articles on the various countries of West Africa. Although it might be thought that this would lead to considerable repetition, the reader will find that the problems of each country emerge clearly as a unique combination. This lengthy section of the book is preceded by a brief introduction setting the historical background and is followed by two sections which deal with the common issues these countries face: economic development, the design of adequate political organizations, and the position of Africa on the world scene.

The rate of change in this part of the world makes it impossible to forecast future developments in many areas. Can France and her French territories devise a method whereby their aspirations can be satisfied but a link between them retained? Can major violence be avoided between Africans and Europeans and between Africans themselves? Will West Africa unite or will it remain content with the artificial frontiers set up by the colonial powers?

Although these questions and many others cannot be answered here, an attempt is made to provide the elements for an informed judgment with the help of the various authors, publishers, and organizations who have kindly granted permission for the use of materials included in this book. Supplementary readings are listed in the bibliography at the back of the book.

ROBERT THEOBALD

March 1960

A NOTE TO THE READER

For an earlier survey in the Reference Shelf series the reader should consult *Africa: The Racial Issue* by Joan Coyne MacLean (Volume 26, No. 1).

CONTENTS

III. Political and Economic Outlook

IV. West Africa and the World

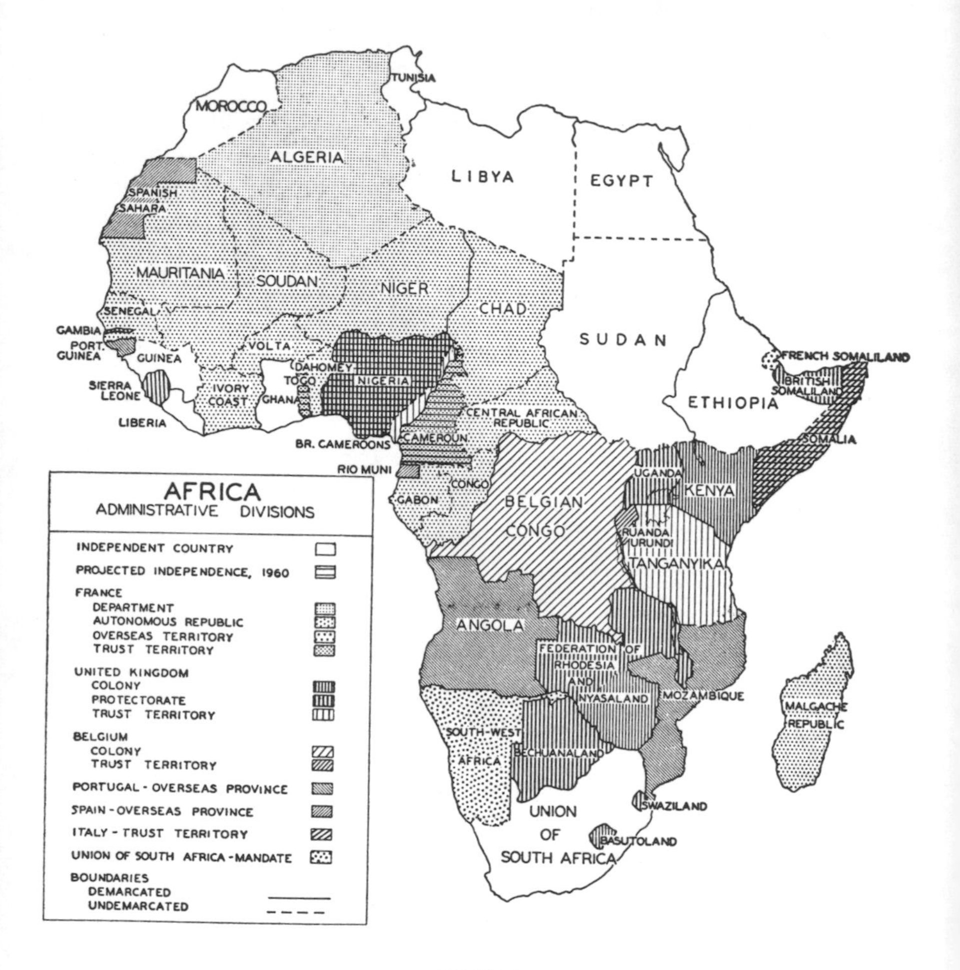

AFRICA

Reprinted from *United States Foreign Policy: Africa; a Study*, prepared at the request of the Senate Committee on Foreign Relations by Northwestern University Program of African Studies. Supt. of Docs. Washington 25, D.C. '59. p iv. (The projected independence of the Belgian Congo is not indicated on this map.)

THE COUNTRIES OF WEST AFRICA

	Population	Area in sq. miles	Population density per sq. mile
Belgian Congo	13,124,000	896,000	16
Cameroon	3,187,000	167,000	19
British Cameroons	1,562,000	34,000	47
Central African Republic	1,140,000	242,000	5
Chad	2,580,000	498,000	5
Dahomey	1,715,000	45,000	40
Gabon	408,000	92,000	4
Gambia	290,000	4,000	72
Ghana	4,763,000	92,000	52
Guinea	2,498,000	95,000	27
Ivory Coast	2,607,000	124,000	21
Liberia	1,250,000	43,000	29
Mauritania	630,000	419,000	1
Congo Republic	762,000	135,000	6
Niger	2,450,000	459,000	5
Nigeria	32,443,000	339,000	96
Senegal	2,280,000	76,000	30
Sierra Leone	2,120,000	28,000	76
Soudan	3,730,000	468,000	8
French Togoland	1,093,000	22,000	50

Data from *United Nations Statistical Yearbook, 1958.* International Documents Service. Columbia University Press. New York. '59. (Figures are approximate.)

I. PERSPECTIVE ON WEST AFRICA

EDITOR'S INTRODUCTION

Africa has often been considered a backward continent, uncivilized, where colonialism was almost justified. In actual fact, Africa was probably the birthplace of man as we now know him and life was "civilized" in West Africa over one thousand years ago. The first selection describes "Three Early African Empires." Nevertheless, life in Africa has remained largely at a tribal level. The second selection by John Scott discusses African history and the reason for the continuance of the tribal pattern.

The impact of Western ideas on African ways of life has ensured that old patterns of life are no longer appropriate. Tribal life, which provided security for the individual, is breaking down; urban living is becoming common and paid labor is growing more important. The problems raised by this development are sketched in the third article by Elspeth Huxley and the argument is continued in the following selection, drawn from a study prepared for the Senate Foreign Relations Committee.

The concluding selection shows how the different nations of Europe have left their impress on the various lands they governed, and provides an introduction to the more detailed examination of various countries in Section II.

THREE EARLY AFRICAN EMPIRES[1]

The Sudan, meaning "the country of the Black People," is the name the Arabs gave to the great belt of savannah stretching across Africa from the Atlantic to the Red Sea. North of it lies the Sahara desert; south of it is tropical forest. In the west the river Niger flows through the Sudan for most of its course, providing a natural link for the peoples who live along

[1] Reprint of British Broadcasting Company talk by Thomas Hodgkin, British expert on Africa. *Listener*. 40:500-1. O. 2, '58. Reprinted by permission.

it. It was in this region that large, well-organized, predominantly Negro states—which at the height of their power could reasonably be called empires—were established during the period known to Europeans as the Middle Ages. Three of these states stand out in history: Ghana, Mali, and Gao.

Why were these states important? Principally because they played the part of middlemen. They were middlemen in the commercial sense: their towns were the great markets—for gold and slaves from the forest countries to the south; for salt from the Sahara mines; for horses, cloth, swords, books, and haberdashery from North Africa, and even from Europe. But they were also intermediaries as regards ideas: from the eleventh century on, the towns of the western Sudan were the main centers from which the teachings of Islam, carried across the desert from North Africa, began to be diffused among West Africans. The spread of Islam had various important consequences for West Africa. It meant the development of contacts across the Sahara between the Arab and Negro worlds, and the growth of Moslem learning and scientific interests. Indeed, what we know about these kingdoms comes mainly from the works of contemporary Arab geographers, who took pains to describe this frontier Moslem region, or of Negro scholars writing in Arabic.

One way of looking at these Sudanese kingdoms is to take certain familiar dates in English history, and ask: What was the state of affairs in the western Sudan at this particular point in time? This may help us to fit the rise, development, and decline, of Ghana, Mali, and Gao into some kind of historical framework.

Ghana

Let us begin with that well-known date, 1066. When William of Normandy invaded England, what was happening in West Africa? Unquestionably the most powerful state at this time was Ghana, ruled over by a still surviving people called the Sarakole, which since the eighth century or earlier dominated the region to the north of the Senegal and Niger rivers. We need to remember, of course, that this ancient Ghana, on the edge of the Sahara, lay several hundred miles north of modern "Ghana"—the Gold Coast, as it used to be called. The main link between the two is that the people of modern Ghana, the first West African colony to become an independent state, look back to the ancient kingdom of Ghana as their cultural ancestor, rather in the way that modern Europeans look back to Greece and Rome. Much the best account of eleventh-century Ghana comes from the excellent Arab geographer al-Bakri, who completed his *Description of North Africa* in 1067. Let me quote a few sentences:

> Ghana consists of two towns situated in a plain. The one inhabited by Moslems is very big and includes twelve mosques. . . The town the king lives in is six miles away and is called El Ghaba, which means "the forest."
>
> The king's interpreters, the controller of his treasury, and the majority of his vizirs are chosen from among the Moslems. . .
>
> The religion of these Negroes is paganism and the worship of idols. . . All the gold nuggets found in the mines belong to the king; but he leaves to his people the gold dust, with which everybody is familiar. . . The king of Ghana can raise 200,000 warriors, 40,000 of them being armed with bows and arrows.

Al-Bakri, you notice, speaks of the capital of Ghana as consisting of two towns—one Moslem, the other predominantly pagan. The site of the Moslem town is almost certainly the modern Koumbi Saleh, in what is now French West Africa, where recent excavations have revealed a number of well-constructed stone houses, with triangular niches in the walls and Koranic inscriptions on the plaster; a mosque; and substantial tombs outside the city. Al-Bakri also makes clear that in his day the ruling dynasty was pagan. But ten years after our reference date, in 1076-1077, the situation changed. The Berber Almoravids, puritan Moslem reformers from the western Sahara, who had already established their power in Morocco, attacked and captured Ghana, and converted the dynasty to Islam. This clearly was the time when Islam was beginning to spread throughout the western Sudan, as much a result of the peaceful penetration of North African merchants and scholars as of the shock of the Almoravids' holy war.

Let us now jump nearly three centuries and consider the state of the western Sudan in 1346, the year of the battle of

Crécy. How did things stand then? The Empire of Ghana had totally disappeared. Its power was finally broken by its southern neighbors, the Sosso, probably in the year 1203. Most of the Ghana merchants and scholars fled north to a new caravan city on the extreme edge of the Sahara, Walata. This captured much of Ghana's trans-Saharan trade—though there may have been some southward migration of the Ghana people too. And Timbuktu, on the Niger bend to the east, was already at the beginning of its period of commercial greatness.

Mali

Politically the larger part of the western Sudan—from Senegal in the west to the Hausa states (in what is now northern Nigeria) in the east—was included in, or dependent upon, the widespread Mali Empire. Mali, the kingdom of the Mandingo people, began to be a powerful force in the thirteenth century.

But it was the great fourteenth-century emperor, Mansa Musa (*mansa* in Mande simply means "emperor"), who was responsible for the furthest extension of the frontiers of the Mali Empire; and who, by his magnificently equipped state pilgrimage to Mecca, by way of Cairo, literally put Mali on to the medieval European map. The lavish presents of gold which Mansa Musa distributed in Cairo, and their inflationary effect upon the local currency, were remembered in Egypt long after the event.

This is how, in the middle of the fourteenth century, the Mali political system struck that most enterprising of Arab travelers, Ibn Batuta:

> The Negroes possess some admirable qualities. They are seldom unjust, and have a greater abhorrence of injustice than any other people. Their sultan shows no mercy to anyone who is guilty of the least act of it. There is complete security in their country. Neither traveler, nor inhabitant in it, has anything to fear from robbers or men of violence. They do not confiscate the property of any white man who dies in their country, even if it be uncounted wealth.

Such a judgment could hardly have been passed on contemporary France or England.

Gao

Let us take as our last point of reference the year 1513—the year of the battle of Flodden, when Henry VIII was the young king of England. What was the situation in the western Sudan at this time?

The kingdom of the Songhai people, with its capital at Gao on the middle Niger, which had been expanding during the previous century, was now at the height of its power. Its ruler was one of the ablest of the West African sovereigns, Askia the Great; a former general in the Songhai army, who in 1493 had overthrown the last ineffective representative of the dynasty that had governed for eight centuries, and taken over power in Gao. Under the Askia dynasty, which ruled Gao through the sixteenth century—coinciding roughly with the period of Tudor power in England—the greater part of the western Sudan was again united under a single government. Indeed, the empire of Gao at this time stretched a long way further north into the Sahara, including the vitally important salt mines on the frontiers of modern Algeria, than ever Mali had done. In the east, Askia the Great occupied the powerful caravan city of Agades, which controlled the main trade routes to Tunis, Tripoli, and Egypt; and in our actual year, 1513, he invaded the Hausa states—including Kano, today the commercial center of northern Nigeria—bringing them, for a time, within the Gao empire. But it was not so much in his military achievements that Askia's genius showed itself as in the efficient system of administration which he developed, with the support of the merchants and intelligentsia in the towns, as a means of unifying this extensive empire.

The influence of the intelligentsia in Askia's empire was a fact which particularly impressed the contemporary traveler, Leo Africanus, who as a young man accompanied his uncle on a diplomatic mission from Morocco to the court of Askia. He said:

> There are numerous judges, doctors and clerics in Timbuktu, all receiving good salaries from the king. He pays great respect to men of learning. There is a big demand for books in manuscript, imported from Barbary. More profit is made from the book trade than from any other line of business.

Timbuktu was undoubtedly the intellectual center of Askia's empire. Its university provided courses in theology, Moslem law, rhetoric, grammar and literature, given by visiting lecturers from Cairo or Fez as well as by local scholars, and attended by students, "young men eager for knowledge and virtue" as a writer of the day described them, from the whole West African region.

Ghana, Mali, Gao: what (one inevitably asks) were the causes of the break-up of these large, relatively centralized Negro empires, and the flourishing civilizations associated with them, after about the year 1600? Lack of natural frontiers—meaning exposure to attack from desert and forest? Poor communications? Excessive dependence on the trade in gold and slaves? The sharp contrast (which struck Leo Africanus) between the splendor of the royal courts and the poverty of the masses? To try to answer the question at all adequately would take us too far. But in the case of Gao one point is clear: the invasion of the empire in 1590 by Moroccan forces, armed with harquebus and cannon (they had succeeded in solving the problems of trans-Saharan transport), was the beginning of a time of troubles, in which the former equilibrium—between Negro and Arab, pagan and Moslem, settled and nomad, city and countryside—was destroyed. As a seventeenth-century Sudanese historian, who himself lived through the troubles he described, expressed it: "From that moment everything changed. Danger took the place of security; poverty of wealth. Peace gave way to distress, disasters, and violence." Seventeenth-century African historians, preoccupied with the phenomena of disintegration and decline, naturally looked back to the period of the Askias as a golden age. For the present generation of West Africans, involved in the construction of new independent states, these Sudanese kingdoms of the past have acquired a new kind of importance, as a stimulus to future achievement.

AFRICAN HISTORY [2]

Africa, the awakening giant, stands with one foot in the primitive past, the other in the twentieth century. Although

[2] From *Africa: World's Last Frontier,* pamphlet by John Scott, foreign correspondent and author. (Headline Series no 135) Foreign Policy Association. New York. '59. p 7-13. Reprinted by permission.

a geographic unit, the continent has little unity in other respects. For most purposes it can be broken down into four basic areas:

1. Black Africa: population about 140 million; includes all of the continent below the Sahara except the Union of South Africa and the Rhodesias; languages—diverse; races—mixed Negro, Bantu, Hamite; economic and political system and foreign associations—highly diversified, but most of the area is still administered by one or another of the European colonial powers; European minority—negligible.

2. The Union of South Africa and the Rhodesias: population about 21 million; official languages—English and Afrikaans, but numerous tribal tongues are spoken; political and economic ties with Britain, cultural ties with Britain and Holland; European minority—a little over 3 million, the rest of the population being predominantly Bantu.

3. Egypt (and a sphere of influence including parts of Libya and the Sudan): population approximately 34 million; language—Arabic; religion—Islam; strong cultural, political, and economic ties with the Middle East and, more recently, to an appreciable degree infiltrated by indirect Russian influence; European minority—negligible.

4. Maghreb: population about 25 million, including Morocco, Algeria, Tunisia and part of Libya; language—Arabic; religion—Islam; strong cultural and economic ties of the first three with France; European minority of somewhat over 1.5 million.

Another division of the continent which cuts across these various lines must be noted—that of settler and non-settler Africa. The former, including Algeria, the Union of South Africa, the Rhodesias and Kenya, has substantial second- and third-generation European minorities determined to protect their property and privileges by every means at their disposal (although since the Mau Mau uprising, most of the Kenya settlers have lost much of their determination). In the rest of the continent, wherever European land tenure and the hostility it breeds are absent, racial relations are, by and large, good.

Leaving Egypt aside for a moment, most of the continent's past is both little known and poor. Progress has been halting; retrogression frequent.

In the Transvaal, for example, remains have been found of a collateral cousin of ours, *Australopithecus prometheus,* who long before the last glacial age perhaps learned simple speech and the use of fire. Cave paintings in South Africa give glimpses of a vigorous hunting and fishing society in that area many thousands of years ago. But when Europeans first came to South Africa in the fifteenth century, they found it empty—save for a handful of . . . Bushmen who had retreated southward before the massive Bantu *volkerwanderung* (migration).

Egyptian drawings five thousand years old portray Negroid people in the upper Nile; but little is known about their habits or lives, except that they were taken as slaves by Egyptians from the north and Mesopotamians from the east.

The Arabs, the Chinese, and also the ancient Persians landed in Madagascar and East Africa more than a thousand years ago. But they never penetrated the interior and had such trouble with disease that they limited their activities to some trading and slaving, often withdrawing of their own accord from what even then seems to have been a forbidding continent.

Flourishing Mediterranean Cultures

For several thousand years a series of great Mediterranean cultures flourished along the then fertile coastal plains from Algeria right over to ancient Troy, in Asia Minor. Egyptians, Minoans, Phoenicians, Greeks and Romans traded along the coasts; built fortresses against inland barbarians; planted grain, olives and grapes on the fertile land watered by rivers running down from the then forested coastal mountain ranges. But as man increasingly neglected to replenish the bounty of the forests, the seasonal rains ran off in flash floods into the Mediterranean; erosion washed away the fields; and a process of progressive impoverishment began, which is evident and continuing today.

These early Mediterranean peoples apparently fought and traded with each other, and did not penetrate inland except along the Nile. They were stopped by the mighty Sahara and by disease. Except for occasional slave raiding, they knew little and cared less about the continent on whose fringes they lived. In the sub-Sahara continent itself, black-skinned men lived primitive tribal lives, leaving no written records and few lasting remains for future archeologists to study.

We know vaguely that several "empires" flourished briefly in West Africa—the Soussous, the Melle and the Ghanaian empires, which periodically came in contact and conflict with primitive Berber kingdoms in what is now Morocco.

Conquerors of Africa

But not until the seventh century A.D. did any outsiders really penetrate into Africa. Then the Arab armies, fired with the enthusiasm of the Prophet Mohammed, swept across the continent, conquering Egypt and surging on across the Mediterranean into Spain and France. They imposed on the defeated unbelievers their religion and often their language and their blood. They pushed some undefeated Berbers southward, where they clashed with sub-Sahara Negro tribes. Arabs, Jews and others also pushed southward in search of gold, slaves and trade.

The Arabs sought to convert the Africans to Islam, an undertaking which led to several holy wars. Caravan routes across the Sahara were traced, supplied and policed. Sometimes massive invasions occurred, as when the Berbers took Timbuktu in the fifteenth century; the conquerors, however, never really penetrated the forest belt south of the desert. And during all these centuries, some white men crossed the Sahara and stayed, intermarrying with the Negroes, leaving traces of their features in such ethnic groups as the straight-nosed, thin-featured Fulani in the West, the Masai and the Ethiopians.

In the fifteenth century, as the Portuguese pushed down along the coast, trading and slave raiding, a series of bitter Moslem religious wars raged back and forth across the desert, shaking up the tribal society of the Hausa groups in Nigeria and of other groups in the area of Lake Chad. And when the Portuguese slavers were replaced gradually by Danes, Dutchmen and Englishmen, the French began pushing southward; the Dutch came northward from the Cape, and the British, inland from the coasts. These invaders found hostile tribes, often cannibalistic, warring with one another, selling their defeated enemies into slavery, and leading lives almost unchanged by the progress in human existence which had taken mankind so far in other parts of the world.

Life was simple in most of Black Africa. Bananas, coconuts and other nourishing fruits grew wild. The rivers swarmed with fish. Traveling down the Congo on a steamer for three days, we passed many little villages where people lived as they had for ages, without ever going more than a mile or two in either direction on the river. This isolation of village from village is one of the reasons why Africa today has so many languages.

Tribal Africa did produce some art; and there are scholars who believe that neolithic culture in Europe came from Black Africa. But the evidence seems strong that in art, as in science, medicine, crafts, religion, language, navigation—in short, across the whole range of human activity—Africa remained until only yesterday at a primitive stage of development. . . .

Why Lack of Progress?

In China, India, Mesopotamia and on the Mediterranean coasts and islands, men, isolated almost completely from one another, during some 5,000 years, independently developed writing and metal tools, invented compasses, built temples and bridges, formulated philosophies, wrote books and poems. Why, then, did not similar progress occur in Africa?

I posed this question to many Africans. The answer they gave was the desert, the heat, disease, isolation—and always these words: "For centuries our most vigorous young men were taken off as slaves."

Yet that answer is not enough. China has a desert; India's climate is as hot and as unhealthy as that of Africa; Mesopotamia is hotter—and was surrounded by deserts. As for the slave trade, why were the Africans not making slaves of the Portuguese and the Arabs?

Racist theorists, particularly in the Union of South Africa, are ready with an answer: the Negroes are an inferior race. In South Africa I was given elaborate statistics on the results of manual aptitude tests, IQ ratings and criminal records. These arguments are not impressive. Too many American Negroes, after only a century of limited educational and professional opportunity, have achieved outstanding scholarship and Olympic records to permit the categorical assumption that Negroes lack intellectual capacity, coordination or manual dexterity.

However, the debilitating effect of the slave trade on the tribes of West Africa was a significant factor in Africa's backwardness, particularly since for every slave successfully transported across the sea several were killed or died in the slaving wars, in escape or in transit. It would be unfair, however, to place the entire blame for the continent's backwardness on the European slavers, for African tribesmen had been enslaving their enemies for centuries; and Egyptians as well as Arabs used slave labor on a large scale as far back as their most ancient records go.

Europe's Traders and Colonizers

But long before the slave trade was stopped, Britain, as well as other European nations, was pushing into Africa in search of other commodities: gold, ivory, pepper, oils and precious woods. And by 1875 the vast continent, like the familiar melon, had been carved up among the great powers—Britain, France, Belgium, Portugal, Germany. The division was formalized at the Berlin Conference on African Affairs (1884-85), although considerable pushing and pulling followed, in the course of which Turkey lost control of Egypt; Germany lost Tanganyika, Kamerun (divided into British and French Cameroons) and Togoland; France established its control over North Africa; and Italy acquired territories in East Africa as well as Libya.

During the period of Western colonization only two African states remained independent: Ethiopia, remote and impoverished, and little Liberia, which, like Sierra Leone, had been settled by freed slaves and slaves rescued by the British both on the high seas and in Africa itself. But escape from colonialism was not without serious disadvantages for these two areas, which are today's most retarded African nations.

As a matter of fact, social forms are relatively good or bad, progressive or reactionary, depending on the historic context in which they occur. In a cannibalistic society the institution of slavery is progressive, humanitarian, enlightened—for it is surely less unpleasant to be enslaved than to be eaten. Similarly, compared with slavery, colonialism was a great step forward. Its contributions are many and varied; and today, in many areas, colonialism is giving way to nationalist independence movements before its potential for good has been exhausted.

THE TRIBAL HERITAGE [3]

Trouble in Africa generally suggests a revolt of Africans against their colonial overlords—black versus white. This alignment is rapidly becoming out of date. The recent riots in Ruanda [Belgian colony in East Africa], which caused the Belgian government to declare a state of emergency, were not directed against whites; they were the outcome of an age-old enmity between two tribes: the Watusi, a race of aristocrats who grow seven feet, tall, and the Bahutu, four million Africans who were once their slaves.

Like all other colonial powers, the Belgians have promised the Africans under their tutelage self-government within the next few years. This led to rumors among the Bahutu majority that the Watusi, whose powers have been curbed by the Belgians, would resume their onetime rule, when the white men go.

The Ruanda riots bring into sharp relief what is probably Africa's greatest danger today—a revival of tribalism once white rule is withdrawn.

Colonialism has fallen into such disrepute that few people recall the state of Africa in precolonial days. The normal condition was one of intertribal war. African tribes are as different from one another as Danes from Italians or Irish from Germans and, like the Europeans, they have been fighting throughout their history. The Europeans, because of their superiority in weapons

[3] From "Drums of Change Beat for Africa's Tribes," by Elspeth Huxley, author of many books about Africa. New York *Times Magazine*. p 24-30. N. 29, '59. Reprinted by permission.

and organization, were able to put a stop to [African] tribal wars. But many of the deep-seated fears and enmities between the various tribes have rumbled under the surface all along.

It was fear of civil war that toppled the democratic system left by the British in the Sudan and created a military dictatorship within three years of their departure. If intertribal warfare like that in Ruanda should break out all over Africa, other newly established African governments may find themselves obliged to impose dictatorships, too. Democracy, in fact, may be the first casualty of African nationalism. [See articles on Cameroon and Belgian Congo in section II, below—Ed.]

No one knows exactly how many tribes there are in Africa, but nearly one thousand languages are spoken and each language must denote a separate group. The linguist and administrator Sir Harry Johnston listed 276 Bantu languages alone, and the New Testament has been translated into eighty-two major tongues. Even in Ghana, with less than five million inhabitants, over twenty vernaculars are spoken and Radio Ghana broadcasts in six African languages.

Many of Africa's tribes are quite large. The Somalis, who will have their own independent state, Somalia, next year, probably number about 3 million. The Ibo of Nigeria number around 6 million, the Yoruba at least 5 million, the Baluba of the Congo 3.5 million, and there are about 9 million Hausa-speaking peoples on the fringes of the Sahara. . . .

Today the very word "tribe," because of its association with the primitive and savage, is shunned by the new African leaders. So sensitive are they that a Nigerian writer has suggested it should be applied only to small, backward groups "running at most into a few thousands"—which would exclude most African peoples. Nothing insults an educated African more than to refer to tribal customs, and to ask what tribe such a man belongs to is to drop a very heavy brick indeed.

I talked not long ago with a peasant in a remote region, who explained how he was working his small farm. He was proud of his improved bull, his homemade cattle shed and the corrugated iron with which he had roofed his new hut. "White men used to come and photograph us as if we were gorillas," he said. "Now I hope they will see that we are human beings like everyone else."

This is the mainspring of the educated African's revolt against tribalism—the deep, desperate wish to be the same as everybody else, to join the twentieth century as full members.

If you wear beads, wrap your limbs in copper wire, plug your nose or lips, stretch your lobes, cut cicatricial patterns on your flesh, you belong to a past your children intend to bury. The young man of today pictures himself in a collar and tie and pin-stripe suit at the desk of a company or Government office—or, better yet, as a lawyer or politician who can talk back to white men on equal terms or even give them orders as their superior.

Thus, tribal customs are dying, but not as fast as those who have outgrown them would like to believe. This summer I encountered, in a little store way out in the bush, a skin-clad young woman in a wide ruff of beads, her legs and arms encased in coils of wire, escorted by her husband who wore feathers in his mud-packed hair and a metal cylinder stuck through his upper lip. She stared at me so much that I asked, through an interpreter, if anything was wrong, "No," he replied, "there is nothing wrong, it is only that she has never seen a European before." Yet we were within a day's drive of Nairobi [capital of Kenya] with its hothouse politics and traffic jams, its drive-in cinemas and parades for freedom based on "one-man-one-vote."

Though skins and beads have all but given way to dresses and trousers, many traditional customs remain. Bride-price, for example—the custom by which a man pays his future father-in-law a sum to compensate for the loss of a daughter—is still practiced. Payments used to be made mainly in cattle, or in beer and hoes. Now cash often replaces cows.

A British governor in South Africa, many years ago, made illegal what he called "the sin of buying wives." Africans do not look at it like that. The payment is a guarantee of the young man's good faith, on the one hand, and of the girl's stability, on the other—if she misbehaves her father must refund it. They disapprove of the white people's easy divorces.

This summer, too, I met an African girl who was especially attractive. She was about twenty-three, spoke English well, was nicely dressed, had trained as a nurse and had charming manners. She lived in a small town, in a way still extremely uncommon anywhere in Africa—as a bachelor girl, earning her living as a clerk. A white woman friend of hers told me that she was a keen Christian and that her moral code was strict.

Her life seemed to me desperately lonely. Her girl-friends were all married, with their own families. She never went out with boys. Outside the few big cities, young men don't take out girls unless they are prostitutes. The bubbling spirit of all African girls I've ever met seemed crushed and stilled in her. Why, I asked, hadn't she married?

"It's a tragedy," said her white woman friend. "Because she's a Christian, she refused to be circumcised, and now none of the young men will have her. Even teachers and clerks, the educated ones." Girls of her tribe are still circumcised (clitoridectomy) at 12 or 13, even those at boarding school who must come home to face this ordeal during the holidays. They are glad to undergo it, for they know that if they don't their own people will look on them as outcasts for the rest of their lives.

Once, in West Africa, I met an oldish man being pushed along a forest path in a so-called "bush chair." He was on the way to visit a famous witch doctor. What about the modern hospital near his home? Oh, yes, he'd tried that; London-trained doctors there had cured his fever but he still had stomach trouble, so he was going to give the native doctors a chance.

In Lagos, fast-growing capital of Nigeria, there are glass-fronted stores that sell anything from Cadillacs to Paris hats; just a few paces away, in the market, you may buy a withered monkey's skull, dried bats' wings and nameless claws to make you a potion as eerie as anything cooked up by Macbeth's witches.

And there is a darker side of African magic that doesn't often emerge into the open. A recent outbreak of ritual murders in Basutoland, conducted with appalling cruelty, resulted in the uncovering of scores of other such crimes. They had been committed to obtain parts of living bodies for "medicines" used, among other things, to bring success in college examinations. Nearly seventy people have been executed for their part in these murders, one of which was largely performed by a fully trained hospital doctor.

Although journalists and other visitors have stressed these more sensational rituals, not all tribal customs are bad, by any means. In addition, they vary so considerably from place to place that no single pattern will fit all tribes. . . .

But one thing that almost all tribes have in common is a sense of closeness. Almost everyone is a relation, however distant, of everyone else, and no self-respecting African would let a fellow tribesman go hungry. For centuries Africans have got along very well without any state provisions for old age, sickness, widowhood, orphans or mental illness, because the family looked after its needy or afflicted members.

The tribe has always formed a compact, self-sustaining unit. Its members gave absolute loyalty to their chief, and whatever he said was obeyed without argument. But as a rule the chief himself was not dictatorial. He embodied the will of the tribe; he did not impose his own will upon it—or if he did he was generally thrown out. Among the Yoruba, for example, if a chief found a parrot's egg in his doorway he knew that he had gone too far and his only course was to disappear into the bush and commit suicide.

Each tribe had its own territory, rites, history, legends and beliefs. No tribesman ever felt alone or unwanted and no woman ever lacked a husband and the protection of her husband's clan. To anyone who deviated from the norm or challenged its authority, the tribe could be ruthless. As a result, there were few rebels in tribal society.

All this was shaken by the European decision to establish democracy. Many tribes are in themselves democratic in certain ways; but their methods of government by elders and chiefs could not be adapted to a system of universal suffrage wherein young men have an equal say with elders, women with men, the chief has no function, and people are elected to political office instead of holding it by virtue of age or similar criterion.

So tribalism has been busted wide open by the democratic system which the Europeans set up and which they propose to hand over when they relinquish authority. But there has been very little time to solidify the democratic system and to train the people in its use. Major reforms have been made in Africa only in the past fifteen years. The consequence is that, although tribalism, as such, is declining and being replaced by elected councils, parliaments and national assemblies, you do not have to dig very deep to find many of the tribal loyalties that have existed for centuries, waiting for a chance to emerge. . . .

In short, two contrary forces are at work on Africans today. One is the tribal spirit which urges divided people to reunite under their own leaders and develop their own particular cultures. The other is the antitribal force of African nationalism —a force fed by the nationalist leaders, who are making a deliberate, full-scale effort to smash the tribal system to smithereens.

So long as freedom is the goal, this force fuses tribal groups together in a common aim. But once freedom is achieved, the nationalists' real troubles begin. Tribal groups start to assert themselves again and ancient jealousies and hatreds are revived.

By whipping up national pride and loyalty, the nationalist leaders may create a spirit of aggression that they will later be unable to control. Or the leaders may find power a heady draught and drink so much of it that they will turn into dictators. Or, finally, they may fail in their attempts to suppress tribalism, and in this case freedom could lead straight to civil war.

These are dangers: but, of course, no one expects a great continent of 225 million people, which for the first time has joined its history to the rest of the world's, to undergo a revolution without trouble. Tribalism, the ancient way of life in Africa, is in transition. No one can say whether it will vanish into a national melting pot or endure as the focus of new cultures—only that it is changing fast, and that, either way, it cannot ever again be just what it was.

Despite survival in backwaters, primitive customs are disappearing from the continent almost as fast as its wild animals. The spear, the ostrich feather, the juju mask, the thumping dance with naked breasts and swinging monkeytails—all these soon will be as extinct as the redskin stockade and the pony express. And not until this is so will modern nationalist leaders be satisfied.

SOCIAL CHANGE IN AFRICA [4]

Africa, like other continents, manifests the post-World War II phenomenon of urban development. By 1957 its sub-Saharan portion alone numbered 35 cities of more than 100,000 inhabitants. In western Africa, notably that part included in the belt lying directly south of the Sahara, cities have long been known, and the urban tradition in attenuated form extended southeastward into the Congo. In eastern and southern Africa, however, the city is an entirely new thing.

These figures are impressive when we recall that most African cities did not exist a half century ago. The newer centers have broad avenues and multistoried public and business buildings, built in modern architectural style. The more picturesque older centers, such as Kano or Lagos, show strong trends toward modernization. Growth has been rapid:

> Dakar from 30,000 in 1926 to 230,000 in 1955;
> Conakry from 13,000 in 1936 to 50,000 in 1951;
> Abidjan from 17,000 in 1936 to 127,000 in 1955;
> Kumasi from 18,853 in 1911 to 75,000 in 1955;
> Ibadan from 387,173 in 1931 to 459,196 in 1952;
> Leopoldville from 39,531 in 1930 to 299,806 in 1955;
> Nairobi from 13,145 in 1927 to 75,227 in 1948;
> Salisbury from 25,594 in 1931 to 167,630 in 1956;
> and Johannesburg from 282,971 in 1921 to 1,030,200 in 1957.

Nowhere has the racial factor had greater impact than in the urban setting, where differentials in standards of living are given their most emphatic expression. Africans and Europeans

[4] From *United States Foreign Policy: Africa; a Study,* prepared at the request of the Senate Committee on Foreign Relations, by Northwestern University Program of African Studies. United States. Senate. Committee on Foreign Relations. 86th Congress, 1st session. Supt. of Docs. Washington 25, D.C. '59. p 35-9.

in the Union [of South Africa], the Federation [of Rhodesia and Nyasaland], the Congo, and East Africa have by law been restricted to different parts of the cities, and as effectively by custom and economic status in Angola and Mozambique. The pattern of racial segregation in West Africa is rapidly changing, the differentials coming increasingly to reflect economic status or official position without reference to race.

In the multiracial societies, the strong police controls exerted over the African urban populations are a continuous source of friction. They are at the base of the pass laws of the Union, the Federation, Kenya, the Portuguese territories and, until recently, the Congo. In a number of these countries, Africans cannot own urban plots, and only in special circumstances may they build their own houses. The African quarters are so administered that essential controls rest in non-African hands, and Africans have limited opportunity for the exercise of initiative or enterprise. In the Union, African tenure is at the pleasure of the location superintendent. Sociologists are agreed that this planned uncertainty exacerbates the tensions and hostilities of African city dwellers in multiracial societies, and leads to aggressions both against fellow Africans and the group in power. Everywhere in these regions of sub-Saharan Africa the African is in the city, but not of it.

It is important that the nature of the social pathology of African urban centers be understood for what it is. That is, it is urban as well as African, since in many aspects the problems of these African cities are no different from those of modern cities in the older industralized countries. We must also recognize the variation in the forms of urban pathology found over the continent, and the special situations out of which the differences arise. Lagos has its juvenile delinquents as well as Johannesburg; both are phenomena of urbanization. Yet their incidence and nature differ sharply, and this may be referred to differences in the position of Africans in Nigerian and South African cities. For example, it has been estimated that in South Africa, one out of every four Africans is arrested yearly, mainly because of lack of proper identification or other papers.

Industrialization in Africa does not accompany urbanization to the extent found in Europe and the United States. In Africa, because of the nature of the colonial economic system under which the extractive industries have a primary position, cities tend to be centers of trade and administration, with the largest industrial developments centering about mines or hydroelectric projects. The logic of the city is making itself felt, however, and centers such as Abidjan or Leopoldville or Bulawayo have become important for their manufacturing enterprises. Where mineral resources can be exploited near the cities, as with Johannesburg, literally built on top of the gold mines, or Elisabethville, in the heart of the Katanga, the association makes for continuous interaction and mutual stimulation.

The principal problems of industrialization in sub-Sahara Africa are those of any other technologically underdeveloped area. Insofar as they have to do with the extraction of raw materials, the question of transport overseas is critical; this is why the railroads of Africa run almost entirely from coastal ports inland. The availability of power also enters. Financing, which for the most part has come from outside, will have to continue to do so as long as the internal reserves of capital cannot supply the means to support ventures of major magnitude. This economic triad—communication, power, capital—brings the problem of development back to the ever-present political level.

Further matters of importance, however, involve the human factor. The first of these has to do with the size of the internal market, and is closely tied to adjustments in consumption patterns as Africans' wants move from handicraft to mass production commodities. A second has to do with the labor pool, especially the development of workers who are accustomed to the rhythm of the industrial effort and are prepared to accept its discipline. The rise of an African working class has posed many questions that are reminiscent of the industrial revolution elsewhere. These problems in Africa were originally phrased in terms of detribalization, but this has been found unacceptable in the light of later analysis.

Labor

The changes in the life of the urban African worker are far-reaching. The fact that the African does not ordinarily, and in South Africa may not, bring his family to the city produces an urban labor pool largely of migratory workers. The phenomenon of the target worker, who takes a job to pay his tax levies, or earn what he needs to buy a particular commodity or commodities for himself or his family, or to meet a specific social obligation, is one manifestation of this. The essential identification of the African worker is not with his job in the city, but with his relationship group in the country. Moreover, where his habits have been altered so as to conform to the requirements of industrial labor, old age comes on without any means for his continuing support. In such cases, which will inevitably increase in number, the assumption that he can return to his village and be supported by his kin group has been found patently invalid. The growth of cities and the increasing trend toward urbanization thus further bring into focus the human problems, which must take their place at the side of the technical and economic factors as of equal importance in fundamental and long-range planning.

Trade unions are recent in sub-Sahara Africa; how recent can be seen in the discussion of the topic in the 1938 edition of Lord Hailey's encyclopedic work, *An African Survey.* There is but one short passage, which reads as follows:

> It may be questioned whether African workers are in general sufficiently advanced in capacity for organization to form effective trade unions, or whether, in territories where the state has assumed full responsibility for their working conditions, such unions can serve a useful purpose.

Nineteen years later, in the revised edition of 1957, the subject received fifteen pages, and the year-to-year developments in the short time that has elapsed would need much more extensive treatment.

Until a few years ago, effective labor unions for Africans existed only in British and French territories. Legal provision for organizations of workers was made in the Belgian Congo in 1946, but these could only exist with the sanction of the government, and functioned under close supervision. In 1957 African unions were given the same legal standing there as those composed of non-Africans. In Portuguese territories, African workers may not organize. While unions of Africans do exist in South Africa, they may not negotiate directly with their employers, nor are strikes permitted. In 1956 the extension of the doctrine of *apartheid* to the labor field made for suppression of the few mixed—that is, interracial—unions.

There are many difficulties in organizing wage workers in Africa. Some of these are common to other underdeveloped territories, such as the fact that workers, unlike in highly industrialized countries, do not think of themselves as members of a working class, while much of the labor force is in government employment, or in agriculture. Special problems, that revert to the ever-present factor of race differences, present themselves in the multiracial parts of Africa. Thus Northern Rhodesia in 1956 had 9 European unions, 2 Asian ones, and 14 African, the latter with about 26,000 members. However, the application of trade union principles, on the copper belt at least, has acted so as to reinforce the industrial color bar. There has been insistence on equal pay for a given job, irrespective of race, but this has made it difficult to persuade employers to put Africans into the more skilled categories of workers, with the result of effective debarment of Africans from advancement.

The proportion of African wage workers who belong to labor unions is everywhere small. Hodgkin, who collected data as late as 1955, states that wage earners represented only about 5 per cent of the total population (Thomas Hodgkin, *Nationalism in Colonial Africa,* Muller, London, 1956). The numbers of trade unionists range from almost none in the High Commission territories to 150,000 in Nigeria, out of an estimated half million wage workers. Here, by 1957 the Nigerian trade unionists had become almost 200,000 strong. Similar growth is found in the French associated territories. In those of West Africa, union membership between 1953 and 1956 more than doubled, from some 70,000 to 181,388; in former French Equatorial Africa, though numbers were small, they multiplied four times, from about 10,000 to 41,000.

The role of metropolitan French and British labor organizations in the formation of African unions has followed the over-all pattern of relations between the home country and its overseas dependencies. In French territories, the African unions were either part of the labor organizations of France, or were very closely affiliated with them. In the regions under British control, trade unions were autonomous, and the Trades Union Congress of the United Kingdom figured in an advisory capacity, sending representatives to teach Africans how to organize and operate their own unions. Because of the strong political bent of the French workers' organizations, African unions are much more active politically in the Community than in British possessions. The African unions affiliated with the French Communist-oriented Confédération Général du Travail, are in the Communist World Federation of Trade Unions. This contrasts to the much larger number of organized workers in the rest of Africa, and in the non-Communist French unions, who belong to the International Confederation of Free Trades Unions.

One striking development in the field of labor has to do with the changed positions of unions in Ghana where the model of the Israeli Histadruth has been followed. The Ghanaian law governing trade unions, passed in December 1958, aims at creating a structure of strongly centralized labor organizations. Economic development being an overriding consideration, work stoppages are to be minimized. The kind of disputes subject to resolution by strikes is limited, and a certificate from the Ministry of Labor is required before a strike is legal. Unions of civil servants, employees of local governments and teachers may not legally conduct strikes. The old Ghana Trades Union Congress has been dissolved, and its assets transferred to the new organizations, which benefit also from the checkoff system of collecting dues. Each industry has one industrial union, the law stipulating that there are to be twenty-four of these.

Obviously, this places the unions under strong government control, and has been criticized both in Ghana and elsewhere for this reason. It is pointed out, however, that an underdeveloped country requires controls of this kind if its human resources are best to be utilized, and that the government proposes to support workers in all legitimate claims. With comparable developments in Guinea, and the controls over workers' organizations already existing in Liberia, the question poses itself as to whether all this foreshadows the nature of labor legislation to be expected in other African countries as they gain their independence. Nigeria, as the most strongly unionized country in Africa, will be particularly worth watching for developments in this field.

COLONIAL POLICIES IN AFRICA [5]

Different policies and methods of administration have been used by the European powers in Africa. For various reasons some have been more effective than others. The Turks and Germans were driven out of the continent at the end of World War I as a result of considerations having nothing to do with their colonial administrations. Both left deep marks on their former colonies; both were harsh but fair; both were relatively efficient. Holland had been forced to leave Africa even earlier. Britain, France, Belgium, Portugal, Italy and Spain remained in control of most of Africa.

The Portuguese, until the end of World War II, were somewhat nepotistic, and are still so today—and rather laggard in accepting new ideas. Like their even more conservative Spanish cousins, they ran their overseas operations as exploiters rather than investors. However, they did not practice racial segregation. . . .

Belgium's Congo System

The Belgians have been honest, efficient, unsentimental and effective. They have given the immense, mineral-rich Congo

[5] From *Africa: World's Last Frontier,* pamphlet by John Scott, foreign correspondent and author. (Headline Series no 135) Foreign Policy Association. New York. '59. p 16-23. Reprinted by permission.

planned and steady economic progress and growth; they have seen to it that the country's 12 million Congolese have shared in the benefits of the developing economy. They have studiously barred Belgian small-time freebooters; have insisted on heavy reinvestment rates; and have carried out an impressive program of railroad, road, port and urban construction.

But, until recently, the Belgians built very few schools; and they have deprived both Congolese and resident Belgians of the franchise or any freedom of political organization. The Belgian administrators have prided themselves on the fact that while their Africans had no vote, they had shirts and shoes—and many opportunities to improve their lot.

The Belgians have shunned the racial amalgamation tacitly accepted by the Iberians (on whom it had earlier been practiced by the conquering Arabs), but have not set up a color bar as such. In theory, they have given social equality to "evolved" Africans; but in practice this equality has applied to very few—and strict racial segregation is evident in the Congo's split residential districts, schools, hotels and restaurants. . . .

British Colonial Policy

Britain's colonial policies have been more varied and far more complex than those of Belgium. For at least a generation these policies have had as their aim ultimate independence for all dependent areas, except perhaps for specific strategic strong points like Gibraltar, Zanzibar, Gambia. Anxious perhaps to atone for its expansionist behavior in some parts of the world during the 18th century, Britain in recent years has studiously avoided exaggerated exploitation of its overseas dependencies. For some time the general directive to colonial administrators has been as follows: "We expect no profit, but will tolerate no loss." While Belgium, especially in the early days of the Congo Free State headed by King Leopold II, and for some time after the colony became the property of the Belgian state, consistently and successfully milked the area, in both the private and public sectors, Britain tried to make its colonies pay their own way—but no more.

One evidence of this policy is that substantial numbers of British civil servants (and all governors-general) administering such areas as Nigeria and Sierra Leone have for years been paid out of the budget of the colony itself.

Britain has worked toward preparing its colonies for independence, and as Indians, Burmese, Ghanaians and many others can testify, has in due course withdrawn, leaving the newly independent nations free to determine whether or not they wanted to continue as part of the Commonwealth. In most cases, the advantages of sterling-bloc services and Commonwealth preferences have been such that the colonies, once cast loose, have decided to become voluntary members of that well-knit association of free nations.

French Colonial Policy

The policies of France have been the most diverse and contradictory. In principle, France has been dedicated to the assimilation of its colonies, to making Frenchmen of its Africans. But outnumbered as the French have been until recent years by their colonial citizens, they have been unwilling to implement their own principle, for fear that France itself would be assimilated by its own empire—a process whose results were proved unfortunate in ancient Rome. One French journalist recently wrote: "The question today is not whether the French can keep Africa, but whether they can keep France."

In Algeria, for example, the presence of over a million French settlers, some of them resident for four generations, has created a political problem which since World War II has brought down several French governments, while in France itself several hundred thousand North Africans have created serious social problems in many cities and communities.

Badly frightened by Algeria, the French have recently been spending large sums of money on development—in the neighborhood of $200 million annually for all their overseas possessions. FIDES (Fonds d'Investissement pour le Dévelopement Economique et Social des Territoires d'Outre-Mer)—France's Point Four—and a whole series of extraordinary financial measures have provided, in effect, for payment by the French taxpayer of much of the administrative expense of running France's immense African territories, and have also built magnificent cities, roads, airports, ports, dams and schools, from Brazzaville to Dakar to Algiers. These expenditures, most of them on projects which are not even expected to render any immediate financial return, are unmatched by any other colonial power.

This is the main reason why I believe that France, in spite of the horror and stupidity of the Algerian war and the serious psychological effects that war has had all over the African continent, has as good a chance as Britain to come out of the present period of decolonialization with an economically viable and politically secure Afro-European association of states. France, of course, may spoil its chance by adhering to its present policies in Algeria. But, at this writing, it still has three great advantages over Britain.

First, France does not practice racial segregation. The island-bred Briton, with his strong sense of national identity and effortless feeling of superiority, finds it possible to refrain from racial discrimination only in his island home. Overseas, he tends to govern through a local elite according to principles of rigid stratification.

Second, France has opened many opportunities for Africans to occupy key positions not only in Africa but in France itself. In the autumn of 1958, in Paris, an African cabinet minister and a number of senators and deputies enjoyed the same rights and responsibilities as their European colleagues. In French Africa, many cabinet positions are occupied by Africans; and large numbers of Africans serve as members of regional parliaments. All these functionaries are very well paid, have their own cars and villas, and enjoy other perquisites. Nationalists point out that most of these men are hand-picked, which is true. Nevertheless, they are Africans.

Third, the French spend money in substantial quantities. Their $200 million contribution a year can do a great deal in Africa. Of course, the money that many individual French contractors and businessmen may make on FIDES and other investment activities naturally irks some Africans. But this does not alter the fact that France as a nation has invested heavily and effectively in Africa.

There are two reservations in this evaluation: France must settle the Algerian war and it must continue to spend money. If France's politicians who advocate isolationism, known as the Cartieristes, should win out and stop foreign spending, France d'Outre-Mer (Overseas) would become a fiction.

After France and Britain, I would rate the colonial powers on their chances for orderly evolution toward some sort of friendly and mutually advantageous Afro-European association in the following order: Belgium, Portugal and, finally, at the tail end, the Union of South Africa—where, I am afraid, horrible violence is almost inevitable sooner or later.

When I was in Leopoldville in August 1958, I found numbers of Africans and Belgians worried that there might be "trouble" if nationalism grew. The Africans spoke of five years, the Belgians ten, as the period which might be required for the trouble to ripen. Actually, less than six months later scores were killed in rioting, which later spread to other parts of the Congo and the continent. The Belgians promised immediate revisions and eventual independence. If they implement these undertakings and aim at independence within, let us say, a decade, they may avoid further violence. [Such is the pace of developments in Africa that this statement is now obviously unrealistic. See "The Future of the Belgian Congo" in Section II, below.—Ed.]

The Portuguese will have their trouble later, if at all. Angola and Mozambique are economically and politically retarded. Moreover, as one Briton put it, "some Portuguese resemble Africans so much that it is easy for them to avoid discrimination. Of course, Portuguese Africans have few or no political rights and are very poor—but so, after all, are the Portuguese in Portugal."

Spain and Italy have already lost most of their African possessions, and those that remain are of little strategic or economic significance.

Brazzaville and Leopoldville

We found striking contrasts in colonialism on the Congo River, in the twin cities of Leopoldville and Brazzaville. Leopoldville, capital of the Belgian Congo, is well laid out, with broad boulevards, impressive buildings, a beautiful mechanized port, a spanking new university. It is an orderly and restrained city. A 10 P.M. curfew restricts the 280,000 natives and the 17,000 Europeans to their own segregated communities. For the most part, the natives are well-dressed, and thousands ride bicycles. Until recently, however, they have had no vote, no political parties; they have no independent newspaper. . . .

Brazzaville, across the river in French Equatorial Africa, is already largely self-governing. It is full of life and strife and argument. Political discussions end in nightclubs, where native dancers whirl and tom-toms beat. The economy of the country, increasingly in the hands of elected African officials, scrapes along with a low investment rate, but with annual French government subsidies, grants and funds totaling some $50 million. Painfully mindful of Indo-China and Algeria, France is determined to give Africa enough and in good time.

With all its diversity, colonialism in Africa has one common attribute in all areas. To adapt Marx's thought, it has spawned its own destroyer: nationalism. By educating at least some natives, giving them new skills, desires and appetites, the colonial countries signed their own death warrant. Millions of Africans, who had never before been conscious of their own national entity—the very substance of independence—now think and act as Nigerians, Tanganyikans, Algerians.

II. WEST AFRICA TODAY

EDITOR'S INTRODUCTION

The selections in this section of the book have been chosen to illustrate the political, economic, and social problems in the various countries of West Africa, and the character of the peoples who live within them. Owing to space limitation, it has been impossible to treat all the ex-French territories separately, and it has been necessary to ignore the Spanish and Portuguese territories which are not expected to gain their independence in the next few years—although prophecy in this field has been made hazardous by the complete change in the position of the Belgian Congo.

Perhaps the overwhelming impression these selections give is of diversity; and they inevitably lead to a realization that there are no simple answers to the African problem. For there is in fact no over-all "African" problem, but rather specific difficulties in specific countries which call for specific solutions.

Another fact stands out clearly. Single individuals can wield immense power amid the present uncertainties. Sékou Touré's decision that he wanted Guinea to be independent was sufficient to ensure a 95 per cent vote in favor of independence although the other French territories voted by overwhelming majorities to remain within the French Community. These West African leaders are trying to catapult their nations from a primitive technology to the atomic age, while devising a philosophy that will encourage economic growth and still preserve that which is of value in the African tradition. Success or failure in this task will depend upon the wisdom of a very few key individuals.

The first article in this section provides a very brief introduction to the status of the countries in West Africa. Articles on the position of the French Community and its aims follow, and then a discussion of the reasons which led Guinea alone to break her ties with the French. Selections dealing with Ghana,

Nigeria and the Gambia follow. Two of these territories will be in full control of their destinies by the end of 1960; the Gambia's problems examined by Michael Crowder are such that early independence is not in sight, although continuing evolution toward it is to be expected.

Liberia's particular problems are discussed next by E. S. Munger, who suggests that the division between the Negro whose ancestors returned from America and the native African is now breaking down. This section concludes with articles on two of the most troubled territories in West Africa, Cameroon and the Belgian Congo, both of which will achieve their independence in 1960 and both of which appear to risk a long period of civil strife.

A GAZETTEER OF EMERGING AFRICA [1]

Cameroon

This is the eastern, or "French" region, of the former German protectorate in West Africa, which was divided between Britain and France after these Allied powers occupied it in 1916. On July 20, 1922, the League of Nations mandated the eastern region to the French and the western to the British. On December 13, 1946, each mandate became a United Nations trust territory, under the same administering power. The French gave their region internal autonomy August 16, 1958, and four months later, offered full independence. Last February, the United Nations Trusteeship Council recommended that this become effective . . . [January 1, 1960].

Togoland

This was the French section of another German protectorate divided between Britain and France after World War I. Like the Cameroons, from which it is separated by Dahomey and Nigeria, Togoland has been a League of Nations mandate and a United Nations trust territory. Under the United Nations,

[1] From article by Milton Bracker, New York *Times* correspondent. New York *Times*. p 1+. Ja. 4, '60. Reprinted by permission.

the French have administered it as an autonomous republic, first under the French Union and, since 1958, under the French Community. The United Nations trusteeship will end with independence [April 27, 1960]. . . .

Nigeria

This will be the largest and most populous of the new African states. Situated at the angle of the western bulge and the southwestern coast, it has as a British colony and protectorate steadily advanced toward independence. New constitutions became effective in 1947 and 1951. There were further changes in 1958; and last April the northern region—largest and most remote of the three forming the over-all Federation of Nigeria—attained internal autonomy. On December 12, a new Federal Government was elected. It will lead the nation to independence [October 1, 1960].

Ghana

Formerly the British colony and protectorates of the Gold Coast, this cocoa-rich area in the center of the southern shore of the great continental bulge received new constitutions in 1946 and 1950. Britain granted it self-government on April 28, 1954, and independence followed in less than three years [March 6, 1957]. The freeing of Ghana provided historic impetus to nationalist movements all over Africa. On the basis of a plebiscite on May 9, 1956, adjacent British Togoland became a part of Ghana on the latter's independence date. Between World War I and the 1956 vote, British Togoland, like more easterly French Togoland, had been a mandate under the League of Nations, then a United Nations trust territory.

Guinea

On September 28, 1958, Guinea, until then one of eight territories in French West Africa, became the only part of the former French Empire to reject President Charles de Gaulle's new Constitution. Guinea thereupon became independent. In November, 1958, she entered a loose federation with Ghana, but the accord has not been implemented in detail. . . .

The French Community

The French Union, which came into being with the Constitution of October 27, 1946, included eight colonies within French West Africa, four in French Equatorial Africa, French Somaliland (on the Gulf of Aden), the large island of Madagascar [now the Malgache Republic] off the southeast coast, and the Comoro Archipelago, between Madagascar and Portuguese East Africa.

On September 28, 1958, all of these areas voted on General de Gaulle's new Constitution. All save Guinea approved it. The result was that the new French community, which replaced the French Union as of October 5, 1958, took in twelve autonomous African republics (including Madagascar) and two overseas territories.

These all remain within the Community. But many have figured in special regional arrangements, and some have asked for full independence. Here is the way they stand in former French West Africa:

Dahomey. Became autonomous republic, December 4, 1958. On December 21, 1959, Premier Hubert Maga denied that he had asked for full independence.

French Soudan [Sudan]. Became autonomous republic, November 24, 1958. As a member with Senegal of the Federation of Mali, it has indicated a desire for full independence.

Ivory Coast. Became autonomous republic, December 4, 1958.

Mauritania. Became autonomous republic, November 28, 1958.

Niger. Became autonomous republic, December 19, 1958.

Senegal. Became autonomous republic, November 25, 1958. With the Soudan Republic in the Federation of Mali, it has indicated a desire for full independence.

Upper Volta. Became autonomous republic, December 11, 1958.

Originally, the Federation of Mali, organized January 17, 1959, also included Dahomey and the Voltaic Republic. Dahomey failed to ratify the accord and the Voltaic Republic formally withdrew on February 28. With regard to the two remaining members' desire for independence, President de Gaulle has indicated a willingness to negotiate.

Following is the status of former French Equatorial African regions:

Chad. Became autonomous republic, November 28, 1958.

Gabon. Became autonomous republic, November 28, 1958.

Middle Congo. Became autonomous republic, November 28, 1958.

Ubangi-Shari. Became the autonomous Central African Republic, December 1, 1958.

Besides the Federation of Mali, other groupings have been established among these republics. Dahomey, the Ivory Coast, Niger and the Voltaic Republic have formed the Entente Sahel-Benin. . . . [In December 1959] the council of the Entente, meeting at Abidjan, announced a "wait-and-see" attitude with regard to demands for independence. The four republics that made up French Equatorial Africa belong to a customs union. So do the seven that were in French West Africa. . . .

Sierra Leone

In Sierra Leone, a small [British] colony and protectorate between Guinea and Liberia on the western bulge, there were constitutional amendments in 1953 and 1956. Further talks are to be held in London early this year.

British Cameroons

No situation is more complex than that of the British Cameroons, the western region of the former German protectorate. That is because the British Cameroons were divided for administrative purposes into northern and southern regions. On

November 7, 1959, a plebiscite in the northern region decided for continuance of the United Nations trusteeship. (The alternative was to join independent Nigeria.) By next March, a plebiscite is to be held in the southern region. Here the alternatives will be continuance of the United Nations trusteeship, independence or merger with newly sovereign Cameroon.

Belgian Congo

Belgian Congo, in the heart of sub-Sahara Africa, remains a Belgian colony. But local governmental reforms were instituted in 1957 and last January, the Brussels regime announced a plan pointing toward a "democracy" in the Congo "capable of exercising sovereignty and making decisions about its independence."

As in Algeria, though not to the same degree, nationalist pressures . . . increased the likelihood of major constitutional changes. . . . [The Brussels Conference, held in January 1960, scheduled elections for May 1960 and independence for June 1960.—Ed.]

Ruanda-Urundi

Between the Belgian Congo and Tanganyika lies Ruanda-Urundi, from 1878 to 1918 a part of German East Africa. The separate but adjoining kingdoms of Ruanda and Urundi were mandated to Belgium by the League of Nations. On December 13, 1946, they were made a United Nations trust territory under Belgian administration. In Ruanda last November, the Watusi and Bahutu tribes renewed an old conflict; and 124 lives were lost. In the course of the emergency, Belgium announced a plan whereby Ruanda-Urundi would be less subordinated to the Belgian Congo. Separate elections in Ruanda and Urundi are scheduled for the first half of this year. . . .

Liberia and Gambia

Liberia, between Sierra Leone and the Ivory Coast, remains an independent republic. William V. S. Tubman has been President since May 6, 1943.

There has been no significant change in the status of Gambia, oldest and smallest British colony in Africa. Situated just below Dakar at the westernmost point of the bulge, the colony held its first general elections in 1954.

Portuguese Territories

Of all the dependent territories, those touched least by nationalist movements have been those controlled by Portugal. Since June 11, 1951, Angola, between the Congo and South-West Africa, and Mozambique (Portuguese East Africa) south of Tanganyika, have been technically overseas provinces of Portugal. The enclave of Cabinda, separated from northern Angola by a strip of the Belgian Congo, is administered as an autonomous district of Angola. Portuguese Guinea, just below Gambia, and the islands of Sao Tome and Principe, in the Gulf of Guinea, are also overseas provinces. In each case, a governor is responsible to the Minister for Overseas Provinces in Lisbon.

FRENCH WEST AFRICA [2]

For the average American the words "French colonial policy" conjure up a confused vision of guerrilla warfare, economic exploitation, political paralysis, resentful native nationalism, and subversive Communist penetration. Whatever may be the truth or falseness of this picture in reference to Indo-China or Algeria, it is totally inapplicable to French West Africa.

In this happier portion of the globe, twenty million natives inhabiting an area three-fifths the size of the United States have found French colonial policy to be generous and imaginative. In the fifteen years since French West Africa was "liberated" by Anglo-American forces, French economic aid has spurred an unprecedented economic "boom," while political rights have been granted to the natives faster than they have asked for them. . . .

[2] From article by Carroll Quigley, professor of European history, School of Foreign Service, Georgetown University. *Current History.* 34:91-8. F. '58. Reprinted by permission.

French West Africa, known . . . as A.O.F. (Afrique Occidentale Française), occupies the southern and central portions of the great bulge of west Africa. Its 1.8 million square miles form a federation of eight territories whose federal capital is at Dakar. [The states which were part of French West Africa now form part of the French Community. See "A Gazetteer of Emerging Africa," in this section above.—Ed.]

Although French West Africa extends over 22° of latitude and 33° of longitude, most of its area is in the less accessible interior. Much of the coastline, including the better ports and the mouths of the more important rivers, is not possessed by France. These foreign enclaves, pinned to the coast by surrounding French territory, include areas controlled by Spain, Portugal and Britain and the two independent states of Liberia and Ghana. The coastline left in French hands consists, to a large extent, of swamps and mangrove thickets on the southern shore and sand bars harassed by crashing surf on the western shore.

The best natural port . . . is Dakar at the west-most point of the bulge of Africa. In the interior the chief commercial water ways are the Senegal River and the Niger (which reaches the sea in British territory), but the value of these is much reduced by seasonal rainfall which offers flooding rapids in summer and shifting sandbars in winter.

The rainfall generally diminishes from south to north in West Africa. In the south, where it falls throughout the year, it supports evergreen jungle. Further north, where it falls only in summer, it supports savannah parklands whose trees drop their leaves in winter. Continuing northward, as the dry season lengthens and the rainfall finally becomes uncertain or lacking, grassy savannah gradually gives way to the Sahara Desert.

The people of this area, largely Negroid, lived for centuries in tribes and family units which functioned as groups, cultivating in common the soil to which they were linked by elaborate religious and social bonds. In these groups, roles and status were bound by custom into a mutually satisfying nexus in which women and children, as well as men, had important functions and were, thus, esteemed and self-respecting.

The whole was tied together by animistic and polytheistic religious ideas closely related to the earth and with complex magical and ceremonial elements. The essential feature of the system was its sense of community emphasized by the fact that an individual could assure his future by cooperating with the system, not by resisting or changing it nor by competition with his fellows.

Over the centuries this system has retained its chief features of diverse local customs even under the impact of powerful outside influences. Berbers and Arabs from the north brought to the area grassland pastoralism and, later, Moslem monotheism; European whites brought the ravages of slave-hunting and ultimately the imposed peace and order of European domination.

But well into the twentieth century the peasant villages of Black Africa retained their local diversity, their solid foundation of status and custom, and their relative self-sufficient economic life. One of the consequences of this way of life is that even today the people of French West Africa speak over one hundred different languages and can often communicate with each other only in French.

At the present time, these local peasant cultures along with the pastoralism of the northern grasslands are being completely transformed by European influences, above all by commercialism, European ideas and modern technology. Commercialism with price relationships is replacing customary economic and social relationships. European ideas are replacing such traditional loyalties as the family, and traditional authorities like chiefs and witch-doctors.

European urgency and its hectic sense of time are destroying the older, timeless and ceremonious way of life, while European technology has brought greater mobility, speedy communication and increased production. These forces began to work more than a generation ago, but have been much accelerated in the last fifteen years. In this decade and a half the disruptions of World War II have been followed by the corrosive intrusion of new ideas and by the stimulation of high world prices for such West African products as cocoa, cotton, vegetable oils and minerals.

Economic Changes

Before the liberation of France itself in 1944, plans were made for building up the economic and social foundations of France Overseas. In the ten years, 1948-1958, FIDES [agency for distributing aid to French possessions overseas] has made a direct public investment of almost two billion dollars. Almost a fifth of this has gone to French West Africa. At the same time, private investment has been encouraged by a number of financial, fiscal, and commercial regulations. The West African franc was made freely convertible with the metropolitan franc but was worth twice as much. This exchange was kept stable by stabilization funds which maintained the value of the African franc.

Certain African products, such as peanuts or cocoa, were kept at artificial prices above the world price level to encourage production. Tax rates in Africa were considerably lower than in France itself, and new industries were generally made tax-exempt for the first five years. The French home market was reserved for some African products by tariff differentials. As a consequence of such encouragement, it was officially estimated that every franc invested in Africa from metropolitan France stimulates a local African investment 2.2 times as large.

Much of this investment, especially under the first plan (1948-1953), went into transportation. Nevertheless, transportation remains costly and burdensome. Strangely enough, this has favorably influenced the growth of processing industries and thus has tended to free West Africa, to some extent, from the old colonial bondage of exchanging raw materials exported at low prices for processed goods imported at relatively high prices.

In French West Africa five seaports (Dakar, Abidjan, Conakry, Cotonou and Kaolack) handle 95 per cent of the area's foreign traffic. Three-quarters of this freight comes to these ports by rail. Although the railways have been extended and considerably rebuilt in the last ten years and are constantly being supplemented by truck and air traffic, transportation costs remain very high. Imported goods cost 50-80 per cent more at Bamako on the Niger River than at their port of entry at Dakar, while local products at Bamako are worth up to 60 per cent less than they are in Dakar. . . .

Dakar's population increased from 132,000 in 1945 to 171,000 in 1950, and is over 300,000 today. On a lesser scale, this pattern has been repeated in other places. Abidjan, the port of Ivory Coast, did not exist at all in 1933 and had no adequate harbor until 1951; its population was 46,000 in 1945 and must be twice that now. In the five years 1949-1954 the physical volume of exports from A.O.F. to non-French destinations increased 126 per cent, while the volume of imports from the same areas in the same period rose 79 per cent. In four years (1951-1955) freight exported from Conakry increased from 250,000 to 1.52 million tons.

Generally speaking, agricultural research has sought new methods which could be fitted into the existing patterns of peasant farming. In a few areas, large mechanical plantations have been introduced, but the most helpful large projects have been established as local variants on the American TVA. At Richard-Toll, near the mouth of the Senegal River, a combination irrigation-hydroelectric-navigation project is already well established. It will, when completed, provide a million acres of irrigated land for rice and cotton culture and a quantity of electric power. Ocean-size vessels will be able to go twice as far up the river, and importing 60,000 tons of rice a year will no longer be necessary. . . .

New agricultural knowledge has been spread by all the well-known methods. In addition, *Sociétés de prévoyance* with compulsory membership were established in many areas after 1915. Supported by a poll tax of about seven francs a year, these organizations supplied their members with seed, information, agricultural credit and local transport. On occasion they built dams or wells and handled sales of produce. Since 1947, they have been replaced by more democratic and less official mutual cooperatives which concentrate on joint marketing arrangements. There are now many hundreds of these new groups. They work closely with various commodity price stabilization funds created since 1954. These funds finance their operations by borrowing from the national Equalization Fund set up in Paris in February, 1955 (capital 5,750 million francs).

The chief economic weakness of French West Africa, besides the chronic need for improved transportation, is the high cost of power. Coal and petroleum are lacking; hydroelectricity is expensive. In 1954 and 1955 almost 20 million francs were spent on petroleum reconnaissance in the Sahara. . . .

The crying economic need for A.O.F., as for many other parts of the world, is a cheap method for the direct use of sunlight as a source of power. America's best contribution to the defeat of communism as an economic and social threat would be to provide the world with an efficient method for doing this. Nowhere would this invention be more helpful than in West Africa, where sunlight is the greatest unexploited natural resource.

In recent years valuable mineral deposits have been found in A.O.F. In Mauritania there are copper reserves of 27 million tons and iron reserves of 100 million tons (of 65 per cent ore). The copper is now being exploited by a company with 800 million francs of capital and should eventually produce 20,000 tons of copper a year. The iron is being developed by a Franco-British firm with 750 million francs of capital and should, in time, yield 4 million tons of ore comparable to the best Swedish quality. . . .

The recent increases in production in French Africa have provided rising standards of living for the area. An official estimate of 1956 fixed this rise at 68 per cent in the period 1947-1953. In 1953-1955 some of this was distributed to consumers in Africa by lowering costs of transportation, electric power, some consumers' goods and indirect taxes, at the very time that prices of African products were being raised in France.

In a speech at Princeton on October 15, 1957, Pierre Moussa, Director of Economic Affairs and Planning to the Ministry of Overseas France, stated that the gross national product of French Black Africa (French West Africa, French Equatorial Africa and the Cameroons) rose 115 per cent in the nine years 1947-1956. This would represent an increase from 231 billion to 497 billion African francs of constant value.

THE FRENCH COMMUNITY [3]

The founding of La Communauté (The Community), an association of free and equal nations, represents a decisive step forward in cooperation among peoples. The former French Colonial Empire which had become the French Union was thus completely transformed by the free choice of its inhabitants.

At the end of the nineteenth and the beginning of the twentieth century when most of the African territories and Madagascar were organized, prevailing economic and social conditions in these regions were such that government had to take an authoritative form. There could, as yet, be no question of self-government by the populations of these areas. The governor, appointed by France, exercised widespread powers. The right to vote had been introduced only in Senegal. But the progressive development of the colonies was planned in such a way that the inhabitants would eventually become French citizens.

This evolution was hastened by the developments of the last war which gave the French overseas territories a greater awareness of their ever more important role and of the basic freedom they enjoyed. When, in August 1940, French Equatorial Africa and Cameroons, thanks to the influence of Governor General Eboue, himself of African origin, were among the

[3] From *Communauté,* supplement to number 150 of *Documentation Française Illustrée.* French Press and Information Services. 972 Fifth Avenue. New York 21. '59. Reprinted by permission.

very first to rally to the cause of Free France, they had an opportunity for the first time to exercise free choice in deciding their own destiny.

In February 1944, the Brazzaville Conference set forth the principles which were to serve as a basis for France's postwar policy for the overseas territories: progressive increases in political autonomy for the territories, development of liberties and civil rights. With this in view, the constitution of 1946 changed the status of the colonies to that of overseas territories or departments and gave them the right to elect deputies and senators to the French parliament. In addition, the French parliament promulgated a labor code in 1952 which guaranteed the same rights to salaried employees in Africa and Madagascar as to those in France. . . .

The Constitution proposed by General de Gaulle in 1958 was characterized by two main ideas with regard to French overseas territories:

(1) The territories were to have absolute freedom in choosing their own destiny.

(2) Each of them was to be offered the opportunity, without sacrificing its individual autonomy, of joining a vast ensemble of nations which alone in the modern world could provide protection against the dangers menacing the weak and isolated and give the assistance necessary for the achievement of economic self-sufficiency.

The territories were offered four choices:

Immediate independence by voting "no" in the referendum on September 28, 1958. Only Guinea chose this alternative.

The territories which voted "yes" had the choice between:

Status as a French department. Martinique, Guadeloupe, French Guiana and Reunion Island had possessed this status since 1946 and retained it.

Status as an overseas territory, thus maintaining the *status quo* with representation in the French Parliament and administrative autonomy. French Somaliland, French Polynesia, the Comoro Islands, Saint-Pierre and Miquelon and New Caledonia chose this status.

Status as a member state of the Community. All the territories of French West Africa, of French Equatorial Africa and Madagascar who had voted "yes" chose this solution and thus became states which were separate from the French Republic. Each adopted its own constitution early in 1959, elected its own assembly and formed its own government.

The Community is thus founded on a multilateral contract between the French Republic (including France, the Algerian and Saharan departments, the overseas departments and the overseas territories), the Central African Republic, the Republic of the Congo, the Ivory Coast Republic, the Republic of Dahomey, the Gabon Republic, the Republic of Upper Volta, the Malagasy [or Malgache] Republic [Madagascar], the Islamic Republic of Mauritania, the Republic of Niger, the Republic of Senegal, the Soudanese Republic and the Chad Republic.

The thirteen member states are likewise self-determined: they may at any time decide by a vote of their assembly followed by a referendum, to break the contract and leave the Community.

As members of the Community, they enjoy complete freedom of administrative decision. By mutual agreement, however, certain specific matters: foreign policy, national defense, economic and financial policy, policies in regard to strategic raw materials and higher education—except in the case of specific agreements—are under the jurisdiction of the Community as a whole.

The Community is presided over and represented by the President of the Community, who is also the President of the French Republic. . . . General de Gaulle was elected to this office on December 21, 1958. . .

The Executive Council of the Community is presided over by the President of the Community and administers affairs for the Community as a whole. Its membership consists of the premiers of all the states each of whom has an equal voice, as well as the ministers of the French Republic specializing in Community affairs.

The Executive Council meets either in Paris or in the capital of one of the other member states of the Community. Thus, its fourth meeting on July 7 and 8, 1959, took place in Tananarive, the capital of the Malagasy Republic.

The Senate of the Community, an assembly of 284 members is composed of representatives of the assemblies of each of the states. The number of representatives of each state is proportional to its population. The Senate debates matters regarding the Community as a whole.

The Court of Arbitration of the Community is authorized to settle disputes which may arise between member states and to rule on the interpretation or the application of the provisions of the Constitution.

Lastly, African and Malagasy political leaders have been appointed as advisory ministers to the government of the French Republic. Their function is to advise the French government on matters concerning the Community. They may be designated as members of French delegations to international organizations or international conferences. Messrs. Félix Houphouet-Boigny (Ivory Coast), Gabriel Lisette (Chad), Leopold Sedar Senghor (Senegal) and Philibert Tsiranana (Madagascar) were appointed advisory ministers for a period of one year by the decrees dated July 23, 1959. . . .

Public Health

The organization of public health services is particularly difficult because of the diversity of the climatic regions, the dispersion of the population, and the existence of endemic diseases.

The first task to be accomplished is the systematic elimination of these diseases. Sleeping sickness, yellow fever, malaria, leprosy and tuberculosis have necessitated continuous efforts. In the past the detection of these diseases has generally been entrusted to mobile units traveling from village to village and this method continues to be applied in areas where the diseases have not yet been completely wiped out.

Hospitalization and care of the sick are provided by more than 3,000 units with more than 62,500 beds. These units require the services of a large number of highly trained specialists since the variety of tropical diseases is greater than the variety of diseases in temperate climates. Two thousand dispensaries, 593 medical centers, 600 maternity hospitals and 41 modern general hospitals serve the population and 90 per cent of the patients are given free treatment. Mention should also be made of the 307 private clinics, some of which have attained international fame. That of Doctor Schweitzer at Lambaréné (Gabon) is among these. . . .

Education

A large proportion of the national budget is given over to education. The intellectual vitality of the peoples and their desire to attain a high level of culture rapidly is attested by the fact that budgetary allotments for education run from 10 per cent to 26 per cent.

School attendance figures have grown steadily:

1946	329,440
1954	663,153
1957	887,145
1958	996,697

The number of teachers has, of course, increased proportionally. In the primary schools, 95 per cent of the teachers are African or Malagasy, the others, French.

In recent years, a particular effort has been made in the field of technical and professional training to provide the specialists necessary for the economic development of these states.

Private schools are highly respected by the people. In countries such as the Republic of Dahomey where missions (Catholic and Protestant) have been in existence for a long time, attendance figures are sometimes higher at private than at public schools.

The development of higher education is an outstanding indication of progress in the states of the Community. The University of Dakar was founded in 1946. In 1957 it had an attendance of 498 students. At the beginning of the school year in 1958, this figure had grown to 1,069.

The Center of Higher Education at Tananarive which up to the present time has been affiliated with a university in France, will become a completely independent university in 1961. Other university centers are being organized in Abidjan and in Brazzaville.

In addition, 6,700 Africans are pursuing studies at institutions of higher learning in France.

Mines, Energy

For a long time the very large area covered by the Community delayed the systematic prospecting of the subsoil but at the present time ever more precise geological maps are being prepared and are at the disposal of prospectors.

Early discoveries justify considerable optimism and work is being done to determine the size of the mineral deposits and the best method for working them, chiefly as concerns iron, manganese, uranium, industrial diamonds, oil and phosphates.

In Gabon, work has already been begun on the manganese deposits at Franceville. A railroad 155 miles in length will connect the mines to the Congo-Ocean railroad and make it possible to transport an annual production of 500,000 tons which may be increased to a million tons. The extent of the iron deposits at Mekambo, for which a 405-mile long railway will be required, is being investigated. Oil production figures in Gabon have already reached 500,000 tons per year. In Mauritania, studies of the iron deposits at Fort-Gouraud and the copper deposits at Akjoujt are likewise at an advanced stage.

With the harnessing of sources of energy, large-scale industrial developments may be envisaged in the near future. In the Congo, the Kouilou dam will produce 6.5 billion kilowatt hours per year for the Kouilou-Pointe-Noire electro-industrial complex. This project alone will call for investments of more than 200 billion francs, *i.e.,* approximately $400 million.

The states bordering on the Sahara will be able to utilize additional resources for their development through participation in the Organisation Commune des Régions Sahariennes (O.C.R.S., Common Organization for the Regions of the Sahara). By entering into contracts with this organization, they benefit from technical assistance programs for geological prospecting and from the mineral wealth consequently exploited. Thus, the oil deposits at Hassi Messaoud and Edjelé alone, situated in the Saharan departments of the French Republic will soon be contributing to financing the budgets of neighboring African nations thanks to the taxes earmarked by the French government for the use of the O.C.R.S. . . .

After several decades of research and investment, it would now appear that the efforts which have been put forth will begin to show positive results. In the last ten years, more than 4,400 billion francs ($8.8 billion) have been spent in the underdeveloped countries of the franc zone (Community, Algeria, Sahara, overseas departments . . .), *i.e.,* approximately 2.4 per cent of the French national income. This represents a considerable sum for it must be added to that covering reconstruction and modernization of the means of production in France.

The Community is now reaching the stage where, after having ensured adequate food and nutrition for its most underprivileged inhabitants, it may begin to make available the consumer products produced by modern techniques. These latter have long been too costly for the low income of the mass of the people but economic development may now proceed rapidly in proportion to the indispensable technical and financial assistance provided by an economically advanced nation.

DE GAULLE BACKS LOOSE AFRICA TIES [4]

[In Saint-Louis, Senegal Republic, on December 12, 1959] President Charles de Gaulle . . . transformed the French Community of the future into an association of sovereign nations linked "only by their own free will."

He proclaimed to a crowd of nearly ten thousand Africans, some of whom wept and all of whom cheered and sang the "Marseillaise," that the Federation of Mali would accede to

[4] News story by Thomas F. Brady, New York *Times* correspondent. New York *Times.* p 17. D. 13, '59. Reprinted by permission.

full sovereignty "not only with the accord but with the aid of France." . . .

A few moments before General de Gaulle's speech, in one of the strongest tributes ever paid by a nationalist to the chief of a colonial power, Mamadou Dia, Premier of Senegal and Deputy Premier of Mali, called the President of France "the most curious and unexpected mixture of humanism and realism."

Negotiations for the transfer of sovereign powers from France to the Mali Federation, which unites the autonomous republics of Senegal and Soudan, will take place in Paris at the end of January [1960], Leopold Sedar Senghor, Speaker of the Mali Federal Assembly, disclosed in an interview. . . .

M. Senghor, the best known of the French African intellectuals, whose friendship and political alliance with M. Dia is of extreme importance, disclosed also that, while Mali would take over the sovereign attribute of its own defense, France would maintain military bases here, Mali would remain in the French monetary and customs union, and French would be the official language of the new nation.

The leaders of Mali have been regarded as the most extreme nationalists of the French Community, but their admiration for General de Gaulle and for France today appeared stronger than any attachment this correspondent has seen before in Africa for a European leader or a European power.

M. Dia, whom no one has ever accused of sympathy for colonialism, spoke to the brilliantly clad crowd of Africans of "our natural ally, France," and predicted that the Community would become "an association of adult peoples in full liberty, equality and fraternity, according to the beautiful motto that we have been taught.". . .

Unrelenting, revolutionary nationalist that he is, M. Dia called General de Gaulle "the statesman of the century" and listed his virtues as "absolute loyalty, indomitable energy, a sense of the most delicate human nuances, imagination and a political ability that is never found wanting."

M. Dia said also that Mali would "establish more and more firmly the ties of economic and cultural solidarity" with the other republics of French Africa, and would "reinforce the customs union already created."

In response, General de Gaulle declared that in three hundred years France and Senegal had "interpenetrated" each other to such a degree that a Frenchman could not be "more at home than in Saint-Louis" and that a Senegalese could not be "more at home than in Paris."

The Community, he declared, will be a free, powerful and effective ensemble. Modifications of its institutions and interrelationships are in view, he said, but they "must not prevent cooperation or destroy friendship."

GUINEA OUTSIDE THE FRENCH COMMUNITY [5]

Since the end of World War II France has been startling the world by the heady pace of its grant of self-government to the people of colonial Africa. Territorial assemblies had been set up in 1947 under the French Union and it was generally believed that the end of concessions had arrived when the *loi cadre* of June 23, 1956, enabled Africans on the basis of universal adult suffrage to elect their own territorial assemblies and to shoulder ministerial responsibility. The power of the white man was reduced to that amount fairly measured by his ratio to the total population. Now at last Africans had the right and the means to determine matters of direct concern to themselves while questions of defense, foreign policy, and other major issues remained the responsibility of government in France. No other metropolitan power in Europe has equaled the generosity of the French in freeing Africans.

But the *loi cadre* was not the end. The revolutionary changes that brought General de Gaulle into power in France also brought with him a new constitution and more rights for the peoples of Africa. Given the choice to decide for or against this constitution, Africans were free to opt for participation in the French Community, in which there was to be one standard

[5] From article by Harry R. Rudin, Colgate professor of history and chairman of the department, Yale University. *Current History*. 37:13-16. Jl. '59. Reprinted by permission.

of citizenship for all people, or for a political existence completely independent of France. The great referendum took place on September 28, 1958.

Before that consultation of the general will, General de Gaulle made a tour of French territories in Africa, explaining to his hearers the advantages and disadvantages of the choices they were to make. He visited Guinea in August, 1958; there, as elsewhere, he made it perfectly clear to people that they were wholly free to choose continued association with France in the Community or complete independence. It was his apparent conviction that the advantages of association with France were so great as to make separation from the *métropole* unthinkable.

But the political leader in Guinea, Sékou Touré, had other and definite convictions on this issue. It is said that he told de Gaulle that the people of Guinea preferred "freedom in poverty to riches in servitude." It is also reported that de Gaulle was so annoyed with the remark that he canceled a dinner engagement with Sékou Touré.

On the day of the referendum 85 per cent of the people eligible to vote in Guinea indicated their choice; 95 per cent of the votes were *non,* against the constitution and the Community. A few days later, on October 2, the territorial assembly proclaimed the formal independence of the republic of Guinea and reconstituted itself as the body empowered to make a constitution for the new state. It accepted Sékou Touré's resignation from his posts in the old government and made him head of the new. Thus ended for Guinea a long association with France, one that goes back to 1882 if one is concerned only with the beginnings of official and legal connections with France, or back to the fourteenth century if one accepts undocumented accounts about visits of Dieppe merchants to Africa at that early date.

The vote to sever established ties with France was a bold, costly and fateful one. It appears that de Gaulle was angered by the step, for he took immediate measures to place a ban on French aid to Guinea, to recall Frenchmen holding administrative posts, and to arrange for the early return of French military units that had constituted the territory's defense. The loss of French financial aid was no small matter, for France had been most generous in underwriting colonial development plans after the war. Between 1948 and 1958 France had contributed, from public and private funds, the sum of $78.7 million to Guinea, which had helped to make the territory the second richest of the eight territories comprising the federation of French West Africa.

Other economic problems faced the new state. It owed a good deal of money to France; it had no currency of its own; from now on its goods would have no free market in France, becoming subject to the customs duties placed on goods coming from foreign lands. Since France had been taking about 70 to 80 per cent of Guinea's exports, the loss of the French market was serious. It was as though de Gaulle were making sure that Sékou Touré and his supporters would have that poverty they preferred with freedom instead of the riches that went with servitude. Actually, Sékou Touré does not seem to have believed there would be a complete economic break with France. On several occasions he has expressed a desire to "normalize" relations with France, and he has even requested French aid since the break with France was made.

Sékou Touré

In a world that assumes that all men have their price, it is important and interesting to look into this African leader who made his country independent. Sékou Touré is a young man, born in a small village in Guinea in 1922. He is virtually self-educated, having had the benefit of only a primary school education. It is said that he claims to be the grandson of the great Samory, the Moslem leader whose military prowess hampered the French conquest of Niger territories during the last two decades of the nineteenth century. At the end Samory was captured and exiled, to die far from the people for whom he had fought against French efforts to establish control. [See "Is Democracy Possible in Africa?" in Section III, below.]

Sékou Touré's first job was in the postal service. At the age of twenty-two he was deep in labor politics and soon established connections with the Communist-controlled Confédération Générale du Travail, which arranged to get him a period of indoctrination in Marxism in Prague. He is now a convinced Socialist and determined to make Guinea a Socialist state. He denies, however, the charge of being a Communist. . . .

As a politician he has had a record of real achievement. He has been mayor of Conakry, the capital of Guinea. In 1952, he formed UGTAN, L'Union Générale des Travailleurs de l'Afrique Noire, a labor organization of 700,000 members with a record of never having lost a single strike. As a political leader Sékou Touré was a reformer, a persuasive orator in French as well as in his native tongue. He advocated improved education, more dispensaries, a greater role for African women in affairs, a redistribution of land. He opposed tribalism and the chieftancy, supporters of conservatism and obstacles to progress and reform. A fair amount of violence and rioting attended all this political agitation and resulted in several jail terms for Sékou Touré as a consequence.

But he was popular and successful. In the elections of March 31, 1957, the first elections with universal adult suffrage under the *loi cadre,* Sékou Touré's party won 56 of the 60 seats in the territorial asembly, a victory so overwhelming that his political opponents were in no position to block his program. He was in this position of power when the referendum was held in September, 1958. There can be no question that the break with France is wholly the work of this uncommonly able, intelligent, industrious, Marxist African, the extent of whose ambitions is still unknown.

Problems of Separation

With separation from France Guinea is learning the great lesson of the twentieth century, namely, that while it is possible to achieve political independence, complete economic independence is an impossibility. Technical and financial assistance for the production and transportation of the country's resources, markets for exported goods, aid and advice on all the difficult problems which have become the concern of independent states —this is aid that only the outsider can supply. Paradoxically and inescapably, independence is impossible apart from dependence upon foreigners whose dictation one fears.

If France had hoped that Guinea would be persuaded by its many difficulties to return to the fold of the French Community, that hope died before it could be uttered. On November 23, 1958, the premiers of Guinea and of Ghana, Sékou Touré and Kwame Nkrumah, signed an agreement "to constitute our two States as the nucleus of a Union of West African States." They hoped other independent states in Africa would approve this action; they invited "the adherence to this Union of other West African States." The Union will have its own flag and will seek to harmonize the policies of both countries in regard to defense, foreign policy and economic matters. It was stipulated that the Union was not "to prejudice the present or future relations between Ghana and the Commonwealth on the one hand and the Republic of Guinea and the French Community on the other." To his needy associate Nkrumah promised a grant of $28 million.

It is a strange union, this one between two states separated by hundreds of miles of territory occupied by Sierra Leone, Liberia and the Ivory Coast and by insurmountable differences of culture, language and history. Guinea has a population of 2.5 million while Ghana has 4 million. Unable to understand why Guinea wanted to break with France, some Frenchmen found in this union evidence of British machinations aiming at the control of Guinea. As a matter of fact, British Prime Minister Harold Macmillan learned of the proposed union only some twenty-four hours before its formal consummation in published agreement.

On December 12, 1958, the Republic of Guinea was unanimously elected the eighty-second member of the United Nations and the tenth African state in the world organization. The resolution was sponsored not by France, but by Iraq and Japan. Actually, France abstained when voting occurred in both the Security Council and in the General Assembly.

In statements made by Sékou Touré and others are intimations of an opinion that France seeks to keep Guinea more or less isolated. Perhaps the leaders in Guinea find this an adequate explanation of the tardy moves of Great Britain and the United States to establish diplomatic relations with the new state. Although the United States recognized Guinea in November, 1958, no official American representative appeared in Guinea until February, 1959; and then it was only a chargé d'affaires instead of a representative with full powers. Closer relations with the United States had been sought. Sékou Touré says that he wrote to President Eisenhower . . . [in] November [1958] requesting American rifles for Guinea's 2000-man army. He said there was never a reply to that letter; the State Department says it never received such a letter.

Quite in contrast to the Western attitude toward Guinea is that of the Communist states of eastern Europe. On October 5 [1958] the Soviet Union recognized Guinea and made an offer of economic aid. East Germany, Bulgaria, Poland, and Czechoslovakia were quick to establish diplomatic relations and other satellite states are to follow. Trade missions from East Germany and Bulgaria have visited the country; barter arrangements have been made with Czechoslovakia, East Germany, Poland and the Soviet Union. In March, 1959, a visiting Czech mission of eighteen persons arrived for an official visit; it was headed by a Czech general.

This attentiveness of the Communists to Guinea's needs is coupled with the Marxist convictions of Sékou Touré to indicate that the new state sides with the East in the cold war and furnishes the Communists an excellent bridgehead for extended operations in West Africa, no faith being put in the declarations of Sékou Touré that Guinea is neutralist and definitely opposed to the acceptance of any aid with conditions attached to it.

Economic Needs

The new state has faced serious economic problems ever since the break was made with France. The country is rich in resources, agricultural and mineral. Until recent years its exports were the standard agricultural products of a tropical country—peanuts, coffee, bananas, sesame, cocoa, rubber, gum copal, citrus fruits, palm oil and so forth. In recent years the export of minerals has increased. In 1957 exported iron was valued at $3 million, diamonds at $1 million, and bauxite at $2 million. Not far from Conakry are found the virtually unexploited rich reserves of high-grade iron ore, only recently being developed. As for bauxite, used in the manufacture of aluminum, Guinea is said to possess the richest reserves in the world. Its exploitation has attracted the attention of an international consortium, whose capital comes from American, British, French, Swiss and Canadian participants. The American firm of Olin Mathieson is said to be by far the largest single shareholder. . . .

At the present time one can do little more than to ask questions about the future of Guinea under Sékou Touré. What is clear is that independent Guinea has become one more area in which the West and East are concerned, with the West more hampered by material interest and doctrinaire misgivings than the East.

GHANA: PROBLEMS AND PROGRESS [6]

On March 6, 1957, the spotlight of world affairs shifted to the new nation of Ghana in West Africa. More than twenty other countries had won their independence since World War II, but Ghana seemed to have a special appeal. It was not only the ninth new nation in Africa; it was the first black African country to attain its independence in this century.

Correspondents and commentators suddenly "discovered" this part of the world. They were intrigued by its assumption of the name of an empire which had been great a thousand years ago.

[6] From article by Leonard S. Kenworthy, professor of education, Brooklyn College. *Current History*. 37:17-22. Jl. '59. Reprinted by permission.

They were impressed by its rich resources. They were struck by its colorful costumes and by its American-educated leader.

Consequently the early interpretations of Ghana were usually over-optimistic. Its prospects were emphasized; its problems deemphasized.

Two and a half years have passed since that time and the pendulum of public interpretation in the United States has swung to the other extreme. Today Ghana's problems are stressed and sometimes magnified and her progress and potentialities minimized.

It would be wiser and more charitable to view this new nation in terms of progress *and* problems and to think of Ghana as undergoing the growing pains that every new nation must experience. To understand Ghana better, it might be profitable to re-read or recall a little early American history, recognizing that we were confronted with the problems of federalism versus regionalism (a problem we have not fully solved in 175 years), that we had no strong opposition party in the early months of the Washington administration, that our government was plagued with rebellious citizens who resented and resisted the imposition of taxes and revolted in a Whiskey Rebellion, and that we passed Naturalization, Alien and Sedition Acts aimed at domestic disaffection.

In such historical perspective we might be able to identify ourselves more closely with the turmoil in Ghana and to develop more understanding of her deep-seated problems. . . . The problems of our two nations in their early years are not identical, but there are many similarities.

Fortunately Ghana has many advantages. In the first place her population is approximately five million, an advantage for organization and administration. Her territory is also small, being about equal to the size of Oregon. Furthermore, about three-fourths of her people live within a half day's ride by bus from the capital city of Accra and no two towns are more than four hundred miles apart.

Although there are deep differences in religion, Ghana does not have the problem of intense jealousies which her neighbor,

Nigeria, has. Ghana lists her population as 66 per cent followers of African religions, 30 per cent Christians, and 4 per cent Moslems. Because of her climate and history, Ghana contains few Europeans or Asians and no Europeans have been permitted to own land. This means that Ghana has been spared the problems of a country like Kenya.

In terms of transportation she has had a small harbor at Takoradi, built in 1928 and recently enlarged. And she has had a better system of roads and railroads than most new countries have had. In resources Ghana has also been blessed. First of all comes cacao which has been a big money earner since Ghana has produced a large percentage of the world's supply of this product (38 per cent in 1957). In addition to this crop, she has gold, industrial diamonds, manganese and bauxite. And timber is an additional asset.

Although the per capita annual income of $150 seems tragically low compared with $2000 for the United States, it is high compared to approximately $80 for the Belgian Congo, $60 for Uganda, and $50 for the entire subcontinent of India and Pakistan. Furthermore there has been some education in Ghana, including Achimoto College, with a practical emphasis in its curriculum. And the British left behind them the nucleus of a civil service system.

Ghana also has several outstanding leaders, including such men as Prime Minister Kwame Nkrumah [see article "Is Democracy Possible in Africa? in Section III, below], Minister of Finance K. A. Gbedemah, the expert sociologist, K. A. Busia, and the head of the civil service, Robert Gardiner—all but one of them in the present government. If the good wishes of a large part of the people of Africa and many people around the world can be considered an asset, Ghana has that, too.

Progress in Ghana

At the time of independence Nkrumah asserted:

> My first objective is to abolish from Ghana poverty, ignorance, and disease. We shall measure our progress by the improvement in the health of our people; by the number of children in school, and by the

quality of their education; by the availability of water and electricity in our towns and villages; and by the happiness which our people take in being able to manage their own affairs. The welfare of our people is our chief pride, and it is by this that my government will ask to be judged.

One could debate at length the objectives contained in this statement, but they are certainly among the most important goals of any regime. How then does Ghana fare by this self-imposed yardstick? Much had been done under the rule of the British to improve health conditions in Ghana, but efforts in this field have been intensified and expanded. As a result leprosy shows signs of being eliminated as a major disease in Ghana and outstanding progress has been made against yaws and malaria. Many clinics and small hospitals have been built in addition to the utra-modern 500-bed hospital in Kumasi, with its training college on the same grounds for 300 student nurses. In order to meet the need for doctors in rural and small town areas, medical field units have been developed and several health centers have been built. . . .

Doctors are still very scarce and are concentrated in the larger centers, but Ghana is assisting young men to study at home and abroad by helping them with scholarships.

No one who visits Ghana can help but be impressed with the gains in education. In recent years there has been an increase in literacy from about 10 or 15 per cent to 30 or 35 per cent. Some of this has come through an intensive campaign against adult illiteracy; some of it by doubling the number of teachers available to handle the tripling of the number of children in elementary schools.

Two institutions of higher learning started by the British have been completed or expanded—the University College of Ghana near Accra and the College of Technology at Kumasi. . . .

Considerable enthusiasm has been engendered for a new type of practical education through the Builders' Brigades. In them youths with a limited education learn useful skills while working on the construction of roads, schools and water systems. The nearest approach to this type of education in the United States was the Civilian Conservation Corps of New Deal days.

Some steps have also been taken to improve housing conditions in the larger towns, although so far this has been limited largely to homes for middle class or upper middle class persons. Encouragement to home builders has been launched through the establishment of the Ghana Building Society, comparable to a Home Owners Loan Society in the United States.

A great deal needs to be done in Ghana to improve the status of agriculture, but in one respect Ghana has done a superb job. There has been a nation-wide campaign to stop the inroads of the disastrous swollen-shoot disease which threatened for a time to wipe out this profitable farm product [cacao]. Every agency of society was used to educate the farmers on the steps that had to be taken, with tribal chiefs and government officials, school teachers and radio announcers, as well as many others, combining their efforts. This campaign has not been entirely successful and the work is not completed, but already it has showed what can be done when every agency of society combines to promote a needed national reform.

Improvements have also been made in the transportation and communication facilities of Ghana. Hundreds of miles of roads have been built or improved and scores of bridges constructed, including a giant span over the Volta River at Adomi. But most impressive is the new port at Tema, 16 to 18 miles from Accra, which is being built to supplement the harbor at Takoradi, to provide facilities nearer to the capital, and to feed into the ambitious plans for the Volta River project. Ghana now has its own Ghana Airways and in conjunction with Israel has established the Black Star Line for sea transport.

Every new nation is determined to set up new factories because heretofore each one had to rely largely on products made in the "mother" country and shipped to the colony at a greatly increased cost to the consumers. So Ghana, like other countries, is building new industries, such as a biscuit factory at Kumasi and a match factory at Kade, with aid from the Industrial Development Corporation. In these and other ways the new government has built on the work of the British before they left

Ghana officially and the results have gone far in helping Nkrumah to keep his promise to move toward the goals quoted earlier in this article.

The Volta River Project

The most ambitious plan for Ghana, however, is the Volta River project. Long a dream or a plan on paper, it now looks as if it would be realized. In April, 1959, the Kaiser Industries Corporation presented a plan to the government of Ghana whereby the estimated costs would be whittled down from $900 million to $600 million and the time involved in the construction of this multi-purpose project would be reduced from eight to five years. [The prospects for financing this project are still uncertain.—Ed.]

Eventually this project would serve several purposes. It would dam the Volta River and provide power for a smelting plant, for other new industries, and for homes over a large part of Ghana. The smelting plant would transform the bauxite of Ghana into aluminum, providing her with income equivalent to that now derived from cacao. The lake formed by the 230-foot dam 60 miles northeast of Accra would also stimulate a new fishing industry and augment the protein-shy diet of Ghana. Eventually the water might also be used to irrigate some of the rich soil nearby, thus adding to the croplands of the nation.

Ghana should be able to provide some of the funds for this giant development scheme. The rest will have to come from sources such as private firms abroad, from foreign aid sources, from private investors, and from government and UN loan funds. . . .

Problems in Ghana

Despite this formidable list of accomplishments, Ghana is faced with a long list of problems. One of the most basic of these is the need for drastic changes in agriculture. At present Ghana is largely dependent upon one crop—cacao, which is grown by 300,000 farmers on small plots of ground. The cacao trees need to be improved and planted in plantations where they can be raised scientifically. Agriculture needs to be diversified, with more attention to rice and fodder crops, coconuts, oil palms, rubber, tobacco, rice, cola nuts, cotton, sugar, sorghum and corn. Poultry farming and some truck farming need to be encouraged. Thousands of acres of valuable forests are being exhausted and timber experts predict that it will take 40 years to develop adequate timber reserves. There are also thousands of acres of land which need to be irrigated if Ghana is to produce all that she needs and can develop.

Closely allied with these problems is the need for change in land tenure and in farming methods. Such change will be difficult to bring about because of tradition and the power of tribal chiefs. Change is needed in order to carry out plans for industrialization, for without change men will not be freed for work in the new factories Ghana needs and intends to build. . . .

Every new nation is looking for capital these days and Ghana is plagued with this problem, too. She vies with other countries for capital investment and she has to prove to the world that she is stable economically and politically to attract such risk capital. Inside her own country she has to combat the age-old feeling that land is the only safe investment.

Despite tremendous progress in health, housing, and education, Ghana has a long way to go in each of these fields. Among other problems she must cope with the diversity of languages and the lack of any national language except English. Eventually Ghana may have to settle for English, as India and Pakistan have done for the foreseeable future at least.

But the major current problem of the new government is that of combining political stability with freedom. On that question the record so far is not too good. The reasons for trouble are not difficult to understand; the methods for solving these troubles are difficult to discover.

One problem is that Ghana now is independent and the millenium that some people expected has not arrived. All factions could unite in the fight against the British and for independence; now they have begun to splinter into small factions. Another difficulty is that the various sections of Ghana have little in common. There is no common history, no common language, no special feeling of belonging together.

Then there is a strong economic factor that causes dissension. Farmers resent the fact that they are compelled to cut their trees to prevent the swollen-shoot disease and they also resent the fact that the marketing-board controls prices and collects rather large sums for a stabilization fund to protect prices in case of a collapse of prices on the world market.

This resentment is coupled with a growing feeling of regionalism, especially in the Ashanti territory. . . .

There is also a feeling of regionalism in the northern territories whose people are largely Moslem. . . .

Closely allied with this spirit of regionalism is the power of the tribal chiefs. . . .

Then there is a group of middle class opposition leaders. Some of them are sincerely disturbed over the tremendous power of Nkrumah and the Convention People's Party. Others are men who are embittered over the fact that Nkrumah and the younger leaders of the independence movement broke away from their established group and gained the credit for independence. . . .

That there have been strong measures by the present government against the opposition cannot be denied. The government has deported individuals who opposed it, changed the Constitution so that it can be amended by a simple majority and without reference to the regions, abolished the regional assemblies, and passed a preventive detention act which has given the government the right to arrest and imprison for five years without trial any person viewed by the Cabinet as dangerous to the security of the country.

The trend in Ghana in the direction of a one-party nation or of "guided democracy" seems to be similar to a trend in other new nations like Burma, Indonesia, Pakistan and the Sudan. It raises the basic question as to how fast such countries can move towards the type of democracy in West European countries—or whether they should try to move in that direction in view of local questions. That is a question on which the most astute political scientists cannot agree.

[In March 1960 Ghana announced plans to change its status on July 1, 1960, from a self-governing Commonwealth nation to a republic within the British Commonwealth. At this time the first president will be inaugurated.—Ed.]

Ghana in International Affairs

In international affairs Ghana has already assumed a significant role. Nkrumah has so far been able to deal on friendly terms with Israel and with Egypt or the United Arab Republic, a remarkable feat. He has also given strong leadership to the movement for independence throughout the continent of Africa. And by his trips . . . to India, Canada, the United States and England, he has kept himself in the world spotlight and strengthened his ties with these powers.

The two most important events, however, in foreign affairs have been the formation of the federation of Ghana and Guinea and the holding of the All African People's Conference in Accra. We shall therefore devote some space to each of these major events.

The first step towards what might someday become a federation of West African states was taken in November, 1958, when Ghana and Guinea joined in a loose confederation. This move came immediately after the vote of Guinea on the de Gaulle referendum, in which that small nation was the only area to vote itself out of the French community.

In November, Sékou Touré, Prime Minister of Guinea, traveled to Accra where he and Nkrumah issued a joint statement in which they declared that their action constituted "the nucleus of a union of West African states." They promised at that time to harmonize their defense, foreign and economic affairs, and to write a constitution for the new confederation. Ghana also promised a loan of $28.2 million to Guinea. . . .

Some observers feel that the union will remain a very loose one. They point out that Sékou Touré is not a passive puppet and will not play second fiddle to Nkrumah. They further assert that Touré has been much more favorable to the U.S.S.R., pointing out that he has accepted a shipment of arms from Czechoslovakia and has channeled one-third of the exports of Guinea to eastern Europe. And they point to the different cultural and linguistic backgrounds of Guinea and Ghana, the former with its French ties and language and the latter with its British background and English language.

Federation is in the air and it is doubtful if Nkrumah will let an opportunity like this pass by without making full use of it in his drive for a West African Federation. Certainly this union of Guinea and Ghana has already had a tremendous psychological impact and has enhanced the reputation of Nkrumah and of Ghana.

Perhaps the most significant event in Ghana since independence was the convening of the All African People's Conference in Accra in December, 1958. This was the first such conference to be held in Africa and Ghana was appropriately selected as the site for it. Meeting under a giant banner which called for "Hands Off Africa: Africa Must Be Free," three hundred delegates from twenty-eight nations and territories and scores of organizations wrestled with such common problems as colonialism, economic assistance, violent versus non-violent methods to achieve independence.

Behind the scenes, in committee sessions, and on the floor of the conference participants and observers noted many significant aspects of the conference. One was the challenge by Nkrumah and other leaders in West and East Africa to the leadership of Nasser and the United Arab Republic. Another was the note of rebuff to the Soviets and possibly to the Egyptians in Nkrumah's opening address to the delegates:

> Do not let us forget that colonialism and imperialism may come to us yet in a different guise, not necessarily from Europe.

A third was the pressure to urge non-violent means of attaining objectives rather than violent methods.

At the close of the conference resolutions were adopted. . . . [See "Resolutions of the All African People's Conference" in Section V, below.]

Nkrumah once quoted Burke when referring to Ghana: "We are on a conspicuous stage and the world marks our demeanor." Ghana *is* in such a position and the world is watching. But as we watch we might well bear in mind another quotation from Nkrumah when he pleaded with reporters in London, saying, "Give us time to sort ourselves out." Every new nation needs such time and Ghana is no exception.

THE ECONOMY OF NIGERIA [7]

The British colony of Nigeria, which is due to get full independence on October 1, 1960, has the biggest population by far of any territory in Africa. No one knows, however, just what that population is. Nigerians customarily make tracks at the approach of a census taker. They figure that his labors can have but one result—higher taxes.

In the last census, which ended in 1953, the census takers did manage to count 31.5 million persons. But they concede that many others escaped enumeration. Estimates of the true population run to as high as 40 million.

Whatever the correct figure, Nigeria is by far the most populous country in Africa. The nearest contender, Egypt, has 23 million people. South Africa has only 14.5 million. And Nigeria, on top of everything else, is going through a population explosion.

Because of its population, Nigeria is expected to become the dominant country in tropical Africa. People with long experience in Africa feel that Nigeria will serve as a moderating influence in African affairs. Most of the politicians here are conservative in their outlook. Those from the northern region are mostly feudal overlords. They regard even the idea of democracy with mixed feelings. . . .

A riot of smells, none of them pleasant, greets the visitor on his arrival in Lagos. It's a city, he finds, of slums and filth. It's also one of the most jam-packed in the world. At least half

[7] From "Out of the Jungles—New Nations and Problems." *U.S. News & World Report.* 47:72-8. Jl. 27, '59. Reprinted from *U.S. News & World Report* an independent weekly news magazine published at Washington. Copyright 1959 United States News Publishing Corporation.

of the estimated 300,000 to 400,000 people in Lagos live cheek by jowl on the 1.5 square miles of Lagos Island itself.

On the streets of Lagos, you see hordes of naked children. Some of the men wear European suits. Some go about in the traditional garb—flowing blue robes. You find still others dressed only in a suit of underwear that some white man has thrown away.

In Lagos, a head is something more than just a place to carry your hat. Women walk along the streets with huge loads balanced perfectly on their heads. Children troop off to school with books—and even inkpots—perched on their heads. . . .

Lagos . . . strikes the visitor as being more dynamic than many other cities in Africa. An American who has lived here for years comments:

"These people are aggressive in the best sense of the word. I don't know how far they'll go, but they're certainly going somewhere."

There is no color bar in Nigeria—neither a color bar directed against Negroes nor one directed against whites. All the private clubs founded by the British have Negro members. White people are welcomed in Negro night spots and other gathering places.

For whites who have just arrived in Nigeria, two big irritations are the slip-shod standards of many Africans and the widespread corruption and graft. . . .

Travel up and down the coastal regions of Nigeria, and you find yourself in one of the strangest parts of Africa. It's lush, riddled with disease and plagued with a gruesome hangover from the past. . . .

The land may be bad for human beings, but it is good for crops. Large amounts of palm oil and other palm products are raised in the eastern region. In the western region, the big crop is cocoa. Each year, those two crops lead the list of Nigeria's exports. During 1957, for example, the country shipped out more than 90 million dollars' worth of palm oil and other palm products and more than 70 million dollars' worth of cocoa.

There is a modern overlay to much of the coast. The area is crisscrossed with paved roads. Schools, small factories and hospitals have been opened. Yet, from time to time, you get evidence that things have not changed too greatly, deep in the gloom of the forests.

Two years ago, for example, an airplane crashed near the town of Calabar. Police rushed to the scene, but local tribesmen got there first. They made off with six heads for use in juju—black magic—ceremonies. . . .

It is this very same region, however, that education has caught on in a big way. Villagers will dig deep into their pockets so that some promising young man can be sent to England or the United States for a university education. As one Nigerian explains:

"The people don't care how much they are asked to give. They do it because they want to raise our country up."

People of the North

Northern Nigeria is a giant within the giant. More than half of the total population of the country lives in the northern region. In land area, it embraces three fourths of all of Nigeria.

The north is as different from the coastal regions as night is from day. It is mostly a semidesert, the outer reaches of the Saharan wastelands. The people are mostly Moslems and they cling fiercely to their medieval way of life.

Kano, the biggest city in the northern region, is on the very edge of the Sahara. The city has a population of 135,000. For ten centuries, it has served as one of the major trading centers for the southern Sahara. Now, it is becoming an important center for air travel. Many international airlines operating out of Europe and the Middle East touch down regularly at Kano. A modern airport has been built in recent years to handle this traffic.

In the market of the old part of the city, life goes on unflustered by the wail of jet planes. Each day up to fifty thousand natives gather there to engage in trade. Camel caravans depart regularly from Kano, bound for places such as Timbuktu and carrying hides and skins, ivory, embroidery and silver work. . . .

The northern region is populated mostly by the various Hausa tribes. They are regarded as basically Negro in origin, but they have adopted the Moslem religion and the Islamic way of life. They, too, have intermarried to a great degree with Arabs and with the other non-Negro tribes of the Sahara.

Prior to the British conquest of Northern Nigeria, the Hausas were conquered by a warlike tribe called the Fulani. The Fulani then proceeded to set up petty emirates or kingdoms throughout the region. A sultan, or overlord of all the emirs, was installed in the ancient city of Sokoto.

In recent years, the British have been trying to impose democratic institutions on the north. Yet, even so, the emirs are still pretty much the law. Each emir has his own palace and is waited on by scores of servants. On special occasions, the palace guards parade on horseback, carrying lances and wearing medieval chain mail.

As an indication of the authoritarian mood of the north, the elected premier of the region—Alhaji the Honorable Sir Ahmadu Bello—is himself a high-ranking Fulani noble, with title of Sardauna of Sokoto.

The Sardauna heads the Northern People's Congress, an archconservative political party that is the strongest single political party in Nigeria. If he wanted to, the Sardauna could probably become the first prime minister of the independent federation of Nigeria.

But the Sardauna is not interested in becoming a prime minister. He plans, instead, to remain in the north and eventually become the Sultan of Sokoto.

There is a tiny "liberal" party in the north, led by young men with Western educations who want to break the feudal grip that the emirs have on their lives. The leaders of that party have frequently been beaten senseless by the palace guards of the emirs. On other occasions, the emirs' men have whipped the malcontents through the streets.

A public whipping of a youthful rebel arouses little response from passers-by. Some laugh, but most people pay little attention to the spectacle. In the north, everything is dismissed with "Inshallah"—meaning, "As God wills it."

Slavery is widespread throughout the region. It is illegal, but it continues on a basis that is more or less voluntary. The slaves know that the British have decreed their freedom, but jobs are scarce and they have nowhere to go. . . .

On the very edge of the Sahara, peanuts are grown on a large scale. In the most recent crop year, the region produced 715,000 tons of peanuts, valued at more than $110 million.

Mining, too, is carried on in Northern Nigeria. Tin production last year was valued at nearly $20 million. The region also produces the bulk of the world's columbite—a metal used in making high-grade steel.

As the three regions of Nigeria approach full independence, it's possible to get an idea of where the country is headed.

Nigeria's relations with the West will be determined to a large extent by the elections to the federal legislature that are due to be held in November. . . . [The Northern People's Congress gained most seats in the election but failed to obtain an absolute majority.—Ed.]

Whoever wins the election, Nigeria is expected to remain within the British Commonwealth.

As far as economics is concerned, Nigeria is not too badly off by African standards. In addition to its palm oil, palm products, cocoa, peanuts and tin, the country has plans for building a big dam on the Niger River. The dam is expected to attract industries to the country. It would irrigate new land and make the Niger navigable by fairly large vessels for all of the more than 750 miles of Nigerian territory through which it flows.

But Nigeria, like the other territories of tropical Africa, is not going to become a modern country overnight—or at any time in the foreseeable future.

Says one diplomat:

"Wherever you look, there's poverty and backwardness. It takes a long time to cure a situation like that."

THE POLITICS OF NIGERIA[8]

[Nigeria] fronting on the South Atlantic and stretching back through rich jungle and grove to arid uplands far in the interior, was formed in 1914 from several separate British holdings. It is a very big place, larger by far than the British Isles or any Western European country, and it has a population of 34 million people, more than a fourth of all the people of Black Africa. It has good agricultural resources and a relatively large number of Africans trained in business, technical trades, finance and government. Among these people there is a strong sense of manifest destiny. They feel that Nigeria's size and advantages should enable it to become not only the leading nation of tropical Africa but an important factor in its own right in the world.

There is only one thing that might stand in the way: Nigeria supports what must be the largest collection of political animosities to be found anywhere in the world. Each of the three main tribes, the Hausas, Ibos and Yorubas—who respectively inhabit the northern, eastern and western regions which form the Federation of Nigeria—dislikes and mistrusts the others and has not been willing to concede much power to the central government. Also, some of the hundreds of medium and smaller tribes feel that *their* interests are being suppressed and have wanted new self-governing regions to be created. Religion complicates matters still more. The southern rim of the country is mainly Christian and the middle is mostly pagan. Most of the north is devoutly Moslem and is scandalized at such radical southern ideas as giving votes to women.

Except for this tangled web Nigerian independence already would be an accomplished fact. There has been no argument from the British about the principle. Here as elsewhere in Africa their aim for some years back (officially since 1947) has been to prepare the people to manage their own affairs, with independence within the British Commonwealth the ultimate and logical outcome. But the British did not want to leave until they

[8] From "Black Africa Surges to Independence" by Robert Coughlan, staff writer for *Life*. *Life*. 46:100-10. Ja. 26, '59. Courtesy *Life* Magazine. Copyright 1959 Time Inc.

could be reasonably sure the country would hold together afterward. Finally . . . [in October 1958] the tribal areas gave enough assurances of wanting to live and work together to satisfy the Colonial Office. The date was set: October 1, 1960.

Independence Day will introduce some remarkable characters to world politics. [See also "Is Democracy Possible in Africa?" in Section III, below.] The most conspicuous, one way and another, is likely to be Dr. Nnamdi Azikiwe, M.Sc., M.A., Litt.D., LL.D., leader of the National Council of Nigeria and the Cameroons, prime minister of the Eastern Region, and universally known as "Zik" (pronounced "Zeek"). Zik was educated in America at Howard, Lincoln and Pennsylvania, came back to Nigeria as a journalist, jumped into politics and emerged as organizer and head of the first big, widely representative nationalist movement in Nigeria or, for that matter, anywhere in tropical Africa. It is another measure of African nationalism that Zik at age fifty-four is its elder statesman. He is a brilliant political tactician, a demagogue to his fingertips and the slam-bang publisher of five newspapers which are boisterously devoted to his cause.

Zik's great rival is Chief Obafemi Awolowo, a barrister educated in England, a rather solemn and intellectual man given to disappearing from time to time for periods of lone contemplation, but withal an extremely effective politician. He is a member of the Yoruba tribe while Zik is an Ibo, and he found it easy to convince the Yorubas that they should break free of Zik's party and start one of their own. This Action Group, as it is called, subsequently made Awolowo prime minister of the western region. He is eloquently a friend of the West in world politics and a strong believer in democracy and civil rights. With national independence approaching, Awolowo has been trying hard to detribalize his party and create an organization in non-Yoruba areas, even in the Ibo east. Zik has been equally energetic—and so far more successful—in trying to build up his party's national apparatus. The reason: each man is hoping to be prime minister of the new Commonwealth of Nigeria.

But neither can manage without the support of the northern region, which contains about half the whole population. And the north is more likely to want the job for one of its own leaders, most probably the man it has already made prime minister of Nigeria's existing federal government. His name is Abubakar Tafawa Balewa, and a more striking character would be hard to imagine. Coal black, with heavy lips and brooding eyes in a tight skull, he sits at his desk clothed in snowy white Islamic garb from pillbox hat to flowing gown. Out of this apparition comes a voice magnificently deep, strong and compelling, speaking eloquently in purest English. [Balewa will lead the coalition government which is slated to obtain independence for Nigeria. —Ed.]

Nigeria's greatest problems, the voice says, is "ourselves"—the tribal, sectional and personal rivalries.

> It is regrettable in a sense that we never had a common enemy to threaten us and make us cling to one another for protection. Now while we try to build a government, an economy, a technology, we must also build a nation. It will take time. But it can be done. I have emphatically rejected the idea that we ought to postpone independence until some future day when we will be "ready" for it. We will only learn by doing. And when we have our independence, the people will feel such pride and responsibility that these conflicts among them will begin to fade away.

If there is another thing besides the desire for independence that unites the Nigerian leaders, it is disgruntlement that Ghana got there first—and scorn for the notion that this now entitles Ghana to instruct others. Asked if he felt that Nigeria could learn from Ghana's experiences, Balewa leaned forward in his chair and boomed his contempt: "I can't understand how people can get such an idea. Ghana is only 4 million people. We are 34 million. If Nkrumah thinks he can set himself up as the leader of African independence, he is *very much* mistaken!"

CAN THE GAMBIA GO FORWARD ALONE? [9]

Last January the Prime Minister of Senegal paid an official visit to Bathurst, capital of the Gambia. This is one of a series of exchanges that have taken place between British and French

[9] From article by Michael Crowder, writer on African affairs. *New Commonwealth.* 37:447-8. Jl. '59. Reprinted by permission.

African leaders since Ghana became independent in 1957, and Pan Africanism made West Africans conscious of the artificiality of their colonial frontiers.

Since 1957 there have been many changes on West Africa's map. Ghana and Guinea have formed a loose union; Senegal and Soudan have formed the Mali Federation; Ivory Coast, Dahomey, Upper Volta and Niger are preparing a customs union, whilst the French and British Cameroons are contemplating reunification. Yet against this background of Pan Africanism, the Gambia remains isolated and antagonistic towards any form of union with its neighbor, Senegal.

Undoubtedly M. Mamadou Dia, who is now both Premier of Senegal, and Vice Premier of the Mali Federation, would like Gambia to join his federation, not only because at present the Gambia forms an embarrassing enclave into his territory, depriving it and its partner, Soudan, of the use of a fine natural waterway, but because he believes that the new federation is the basis of a United States of West Africa, which many feel will be the best way to achieve political stability in Africa. Bathurst politicians receive such overtures coldly, though perhaps there is an indication of future flexibility in the recent decision that as from July, 1960, Gambians should drive on the right-hand side of the road, to give uniformity of motoring conditions between Gambia and its French neighbors.

The Gambia itself is at a stage of its political development when some decision must soon be made as to its future. Political leaders who have demanded a change in the present constitution, which they consider archaic in the light of the constitutional progress of Sierra Leone and Nigeria, would like to see most of the officials lose their seats on the executive council. They seek the appointment of a chief minister and the extension of universal suffrage to the protectorate. Indeed there is nothing to suggest that Gambians are any less capable of governing themselves than Nigerians or Ghanaians. They have a highly Africanized civil service, and an increasing number of Gambians are being trained in the United Kingdom.

The main drawback to political advance in the Gambia is that self-government can never be a reality for a territory which is 300 miles long and only 14 wide, and which has a population of only 300,000. While this small population is almost entirely dependent on the groundnut [peanut] for its income, and its Government has to provide all services on a budget of £1.5 million [$4.2 million] to prospects of independence are extremely remote. . . .

The Gambia has tried several possible avenues in search of an alternative to dependence on groundnuts, which are fetching a steadily lower price on the world market. . . . [But] there is, it seems, no alternative for the farmer, who now receives only £20 [$56] a ton for his groundnuts as against the Senegalese farmers' £32 [$90].

Bathurst politicians are accused of being cosseted from the economic realities of the protectorate and failing to appreciate the real implications of this. Gambia is not a reasonable proposition as an independent state or as a self-governing territory. Yet, as in all Africa, the urge to take over the reins of government from the colonial power becomes progressively stronger.

What is the solution? There is the argument in favor of some form of union with Senegal even if initially it were only a customs union. Economically this would solve Gambia's immediate problems. The cost of government would be reduced since the two administrations could be integrated. The Gambia farmer would receive more for his groundnuts. The River Gambia would be used to its fullest advantage, bringing prosperity to the riverside towns and more especially to the port of Bathurst. Gambia could take advantage of the many excellent research services maintained in Senegal—services which Gambia cannot support because of their cost. There might even be enough money to build roads, which during the rainy season are almost non-existent.

Of course the objections to such a move in the Gambia are numerous. Chiefs do not relish the idea of being reduced to the position of tools of the administration like their counterparts over the border. But already the power of Gambian chiefs has been reduced by the recent plan to streamline the protectorate administration into six federated native authorities, instead of the thirty-five native authorities in which each petty chief had his own treasury. And once universal suffrage comes to the protectorate, as inevitably it must, the chiefs will find their power waning as it has done in Ghana and other territories where universal suffrage has replaced indirect elections. The politicians for their part fear that they would be pushed to one side by the Senegalese in any federation or union.

Finally, of course, there is the whole British tradition, epitomized by the fact that Gambians speak English and Senegalese speak French, which hinders the progress of federation between the two countries. The pro-Senegal answer to this is that every Gambian has a cousin in Senegal, and now that France has almost completely handed over power to African governments in Senegal and Soudan the old objection to becoming French no longer applies.

Is there any other future for the Gambia? The cost of federation with Sierra Leone in air fares alone would be prohibitive. It certainly would not solve any economic problems, for Sierra Leone is far from being free of these herself. It has been suggested that Gambia should have a Malta-style relationship with Britain. But this would leave its basic economic problem unsolved, unless Britain were to subsidize it heavily, and in addition to the long-term economic burden of such a relationship, there would be the danger that it might set a precedent for many other small, uneconomic territories to follow.

Above all, the Gambia stresses the need for the British Government to do some serious thinking about the future of her smaller territories, and in the case of the Gambia it would do well to examine the recent arguments of certain members of the House of Commons that there should be closer cooperation between France and Britain in West Africa. This cooperation might well take the form of finding means whereby African territories can have joint membership of the Commonwealth and of the Franco-African Community.

LIBERIA'S ECONOMIC AND HUMAN PROGRESS [10]

I looked again. It was in the gutter—a green glass, unchipped, quart-size, empty beer bottle with its Dutch label still fresh. The noisy crowd continued to jostle by on the sidewalk. Smartly-dressed Liberians in Palm Beach suits passed women from upcountry clad in what the guide books (when they are written) will call "colorful native dress." The gutter was no surprise. I had expected to find Monrovia's streets improved in the eleven years since my last visit. But the untouched beer bottle was a startling revelation. The fact that hundreds—perhaps thousands—of Liberians had passed by, with no heed for what would have been a desirable possession in 1947, revealed in snapshot clarity the breadth of Liberia's economic progress. In 1947 that bottle would have been salvaged for use as a valuable container; now it was just gutter rubbish.

To approach it in another way, the Liberian annual budget has soared from as low as $600,000 shortly before my first visit in 1947, to almost $25 million at present. The 1947 private report of a leading American shipping company described Monrovia as "a dirty, squalid, collection of tin shacks and mud huts with no sewage system, unpaved roads, no hotels, but numerous little churches. The port is just as primitive as the rest of the city." By 1958 the changes in this same city had been fantastic.

Economic Boom

Despite a current slump in the prices of its export commodities, Liberia has had a fantastic boom over the past decade. The Firestone story has been well told many times and written up as an outstanding example of American management abroad. [Firestone started developing the potential of rubber in the early 1920's, and the income provided in this way was one of the factors that sparked the economic growth of Liberia.—Ed.] The vision and courage of Colonel Lansdell Christy in

[10] From the letter from Liberia, October 5, 1958, by Edwin S. Munger, expert on Africa and director of the African Universities Program. American Universities Field Staff. 522 Fifth Ave. New York 36. '58. Reprinted by permission.

bringing the Bomi Hills iron-ore deposit into production is a saga for those who think fortunes can't be made under present tax structures. His voluntary revision of the Liberia Mining Company's payments to Liberia at a time when anticipated profits pyramided is well known. A nearby iron-ore find is to be developed with joint American and Liberian capital. To the east, a huge iron-ore deposit is being opened up by LAMCO (Liberian American Mineral Company), which combines Liberian, American, and Swedish capital. German, Spanish, Dutch, and other non-American businessmen have also invested in Liberia.

The $25 million the Liberian government will spend this year consists of $20 million in current income and $5 million in loan funds. All in all, the Liberian government is currently enjoying the following lines of credit: $20 million, United States, waterworks, harbor, roads; $15 million, Italy, roads; $8 million, Israel, construction; $5 million, West Germany, harbor work.

The long-range future is fairly bright. Even in rubber there is diversification; Goodrich is active and there is a boom in local Liberian rubber planting (over 1,000 growers with over 50,000 acres of rubber trees). No doubt to the relief of Firestone, its contribution to the national income will, it is thought, fall from a point of over 90 per cent to less than 50 per cent in a few years. Firestone has also divested itself of the national bank, which is now operated by the National City Bank of New York.

Critics—External and Internal

Liberia, however, is not a utopia supported by iron ore and rubber latex. The human problems are now more important to Liberia and to American-Liberian relations than economics.

Young Liberians in the West can be fairly characterized as extremely sensitive to criticism of their country. My sympathies are strongly with them because Liberia has been viciously mocked and ridiculed since the day it became independent . . . [in

1847]. Recently, in the House of Lords, Lord Winster lashed out at Liberia's premier world position in registered shipping tonnage with these intemperate and inaccurate words: "I do not think a Liberian exists who knows the stem from the stern of a ship. I understand they live mostly in the bush." This is in the same vein as the savage satire *Top Hats and Tom Toms* (banned in Liberia) by Elizabeth Furbay and other sarcastic accounts which have been widely used to deride the abilities and aspirations of Negro people.

If, with patience and sympathy, you go deeper than the hypersensitivity of most educated young Liberians, you will hear strong criticism of many personalities and patterns of living in Liberia. President Tubman is seldom personally criticized, but the hack politicians who line their pockets, the uneducated university professors who couldn't qualify to teach in an American high school, and the mustiness and deadwood in high places, come under scorching censure from the younger generation.

Nothing has been more encouraging to me in Liberia than the ability of a dozen unusually able younger Liberian men (up to cabinet level but mostly intermediate in influence) to call an ant hill an ant hill and not a glorious pyramid. Thus, for example, the Information Department has published the statement that a decade ago Liberia had a "tin can capital." And a young educator—wise before his years—wants to end the hypocrisy in educational standards and begin with one really good primary school so that some of the qualified foreign teachers at the university can be used. When a trained physicist must teach arithmetic and a cultural anthropologist teaches sixth grade geography, no progress is made by labeling the whole package a "great world university." Foreigners, and especially American Negro personnel, shatter the illusions at their own peril. But young Liberians who have been educated in America are making an essential contribution toward realizing legitimate goals by tearing into the ant hills.

However, self-criticism or frank discussions among friends are a far cry from public education. In the opinion of reasonable observers, there is less political freedom in Liberia today than at any time since President Tubman took office. The Opposition is driven underground—but don't form too hasty a conclusion. Liberia is not a dictatorship by any means. The government is highly responsive to changes in public opinion, and it meets shifts in such sentiment perhaps faster than in differently organized democracies. An election is coming up. I am quite confident that if the Opposition were allowed to conduct a full-dress, slam-bang, well-financed campaign against President Tubman, he would be reelected for a fourth term by a landslide. In fact, opposition to the government may appear much stronger than it is simply because it can't blow off steam every so often.

But steam does get blown off. The young Liberians come home—some forty a year now, a figure which will double before long—and they find they do not dare to criticize the government if for no other reason than that the government employs over ninety of them. This Liberian government is the best government Liberia has ever had and is more democratic and efficient than some other free governments in the world. But it is very far from perfect. It is staunchly supported, both morally and financially, by the American government. Through its power and prestige the United States can take much of the credit and deserves a good slice of the criticism for the Liberian government.

This is how the steam blows off. There is no pressure—at least not legal and economic—against criticism of the United States. And so, returning Liberian students are often strongly critical (and occasionally in private and in the press vehemently so) of the United States. If this is often an oblique attack on their own government, for which they work, then it is all the more understandable. If the United States blocks Liberian progress by supporting incompetent and corrupt hacks around the President, why not lambaste the Americans?

President William Vacarat Shadrach Tubman

The President was wearing a light suit and had a flyswatter at his right elbow. Where he found flies in his air-conditioned office, I couldn't imagine. He leaned back informally behind his huge desk, memento-cluttered in approved presidential style. When he moved to pick up an ivory cigarette holder, a large gold watch—gift style—came out from under his white cuff. We started off with the referendum and Guinea's new position. Immediately, the presidential candor was evident. He spoke of the great honor of being an independent state but described the "heavy burdens and responsibilities." He implied strongly that Liberia had become independent far too soon and cited the opposition to independence in [the coastal county of] Grand Bassa, where angry voters had turned over the polling booths to show their negative attitude. We discussed Liberia's early history and general American indifference to Liberia despite the activities of United States colonization societies. His voice had a bit of iron in it when he spoke of losing 65 per cent of "our territory by force." The President pointed to the advantages Ghana and Nigeria have in the Commonwealth of Nations. He said: "Sékou Touré will be alone; he and I will be alike in that we will be partners in affluence or in distress, but you can never be sure of anything in international politics." The President recalled also his visit to Sékou Touré a few years ago and the visit of Mrs. Sékou Touré to Liberia last year: "They call him leftish. I'm not sure I know what they mean. He believes in democracy and wants his country independent. That is a good thing."

President Tubman did not hesitate to say that the "primary schools are weak. We are reviewing the whole structure of education to seek higher standards. We have retired over 50 per cent of our primary school teachers in less than two years." But he criticized American companies for claiming that they can't find competent Liberians. He made it clear that he did not accept the delayed and slow "Liberianization" at Firestone as being satisfactory. In higher education he put the greatest stress on engineering and agriculture. Tubman does put teeth into his proposals. Overseas subsidies for Liberian students at the primary and high school levels have just been withdrawn, both as an economic measure and to promote better primary schools at home. This will save $100,000 according to Treasury Secretary Charley Sherman, but will also "make a lot of people squeal."

When the President was asked about Nkrumah's concept of an African personality, Tubman leaned back in his chair, fingered the ivory cigarette holder, and said with a friendly smile: "Well, he's the Prime Minister of Ghana, an independent state, and he is entitled to his thoughts, aims, and ultimate aspirations. But I think a United States of Africa is just as remote as a federation of Europe, Asia, or the Americas."

That same evening, the President joined an informal party of less than a dozen people on board a large new Krupp ore boat: the Liberia Mining Company was celebrating the loading of the one thousandth ship and 11 million tons of ore. The President wore a brown sport shirt with short sleeves, and was in good form. He gave a dissertation on the virtues of Johnny Walker Black Label Scotch. After relating a trying experience aboard a British warship concerning a lack of ice for drinks, the President filled his glass with five ice cubes and commented, "This is one department where I am completely American!" In many of Mr. Tubman's comments, one sees wide experience brought to bear on a canny administrator with a keen sense of his people's needs and motivations. He made quips about the American ambassador beside him and about his ambassador to Germany who is home on leave that were friendly but carried a message. The President also told of being in the lobby of a German hotel and overhearing a stout British lady say to her friends, "If that is the President of Liberia, I'm the Queen of England." Mr. Tubman gave a wry smile. "There was no resemblance to the Queen." Liberia's greatest disaster might be to lose this shrewd leader in the next six or seven years before a worthy replacement becomes qualified to step in.

Social Change

I told Mr. Tubman that the most impressive change in Liberia over the last eleven years struck me as being his policy of unification. He was pleased and talked for a quarter of an hour on this policy of breaking down the culture bar of Americo-Liberianism and of promoting the unity of all the people. Let me quote from a speech by President Tubman last year to a national convocation of chiefs and leading citizens:

> We must now destroy all ideologies that tend to divide us. Americo-Liberianism must be forgotten and all of us must register a new era of justice, equality, fair dealing and equal opportunities for every one from every part of the country, regardless of tribe, clan, section, element, creed or economic status.
>
> For the past ten years we have been working hard for the unification of the people; and thus far the results have been favorable and encouraging. But there are still a few die-hards on both sides opposing the unification program in the hope that one element will overcome or exterminate the other. That is a fallacy. No such thing will ever happen.
>
> If any person, civilized or uncivilized, opposes the unification of this nation, he is an enemy of the state, a confirmed political lunatic and should not be followed.
>
> Let us resolve at this national executive council, for ourselves here present, our constituents and our posterity to make our country a united nation under God with liberty and justice for all. This is the principal reason for this convocation.

While complimenting him on his political courage and on his physical exertions in traveling to all parts of his country by air, on foot, and by hammock, I said, "But, Mr. President, have you not promoted tribalism by encouraging chiefs and thereby sown seeds of eventual discord?" The President said that this was true but that Liberia must now enter a new phase which he would announce fairly soon—integration. Unification was the first step, but total integration of the Liberian tribes into one people would be the next goal.

At the same time, the President stressed the uneven cultural development of the Liberian people. He pointd to the necessity of having two sets of laws—civil law (taken from the West) and tribal law—and cited arguments heard elsewhere in Africa (including South African reserves) concerning the benefit to all of this dual code. But he agreed that tribalism was a temporary phenomenon and said he planned that the Western civil law be gradually extended from the forty-mile belt along the coast into the interior until it covered the whole country from the coast to the interior border. How long would this take? The President was reluctant to say. He expressed frank surprise that so much human engineering had been accomplished in the last decade. Asked again, President Tubman said he thought tribal law and administration would be replaced throughout Liberia in about fifty years.

It is truly dramatic the way the century-old distinction between Americo-Liberians and tribal or bush people has been almost obliterated in a decade. In 1947 I talked at length with former President Edwin Barclay who, in addition to being a racist which Tubman is not, had a great contempt for the "bush people," as he called them. It was a cause for gossip in 1947 when a prominent official of the government had sociologically "passed" from being a tribal man to being an Americo-Liberian, i.e., strictly defined as one descended from the original freed men returned to Liberia from America or taken from captured slave ships. In fact, a high official then denied, to me, a tribal affinity on his mother's side of which he now boasts. Everything tribal was then disdained and preference was shown for so-called "civilized" living, symbolized by cutaway coats, white bread, Scotch, or ante-bellum architecture. The change is miraculous. An anthropologist is having difficulty in making a certain study because practically no one will admit to being a simple Americo-Liberian. The fact that tribal admixture had proceeded a long way by 1947 is not the point—the point is that in 1947 virtually no one would admit it, and my Americo-Liberian friends identified for me (and often scorned) those who had attempted to pass into the charmed civilized circle.

Now this change has given rise to a number of psychological problems. Take the national motto: The Love of Liberty Brought Us Here. College students, largely of tribal origin, are confused. "We were always here," they say, "should it not read: The Love of Liberty Kept Us Free?"

Soon the nation will be celebrating the public holiday of Matilda Newport Day in honor of the intrepid woman among the early pioneers from America who fought off the savage inhabitants of the country, as the Americo-Liberians traditionally explained it. But what kind of a national holiday is this for the majority of the citizens of the capital of Liberia if they are proud that *their* ancestors were the ones that were fought off?

The need of—shall we say former—Americo-Liberians to identify with the country and seek some tribal affinity is linked to their desire to be a part of the new African personality. (Perhaps Americo-Liberians were the last outpost of Western civilization in Africa in contrast with the new African civilization.) This change is a great gain for Liberia. Already there are many men of tribal origin in the government and their potential is many times greater than that ever promised by the 15,000 tradition-hampered, status-bound, anachronostic Americo-Liberians.

Education is the obvious key to release the potential of tribal Liberia. Yet it is in education that Liberia has fallen the farthest behind its neighbors. My friend Jim Johnson, British Labor Party M.P. and a friend of Liberia, recently made a justified, although unkind, reference to the American standards of education, or rather, no unified standards at all, for the 55,000 elementary, 2,500 high school, and 750 university students in Liberia. The appallingly low standards have a direct influence on the distrust for American education found in most parts of Africa—and not least in independent Ghana. The International Cooperation Administration-supported work of Prairie View College at the Booker T. Washington Institute for practical training is a relatively bright spot.

American Policy and Liberia

Liberia is certainly not a "hot" strategic area for the United States. But, it can have a significant psychological influence on American relations with emerging African states. The pressure, especially from younger men, to tweak Uncle Sam's nose until it hurts enough so that he'll pay some attention, has already been felt. Liberian Secretary of State Momolu Dukuly . . . was in Washington . . . [in 1958] and tried unsuccessfully, I'm told, to see Secretary of State Dulles. Understandably, Mr. Dulles was involved in a crisis. Furthermore, Mr. Dulles had not long ago attended a dinner given by Liberian Ambassador George Padmore. Mr. Dukuly was seen by Deputy Assistant Secretary of State Joseph Palmer, a fast-rising man in the Africa field. But all that the Liberians are interested in is that Palmer has been designated American Consul General in Rhodesia. The fact that Rhodesia may be an embassy in a few years and is a highly sought after post, doesn't count with the Liberians. A Secretary of State was received by a Consul General!

On the other hand, on September 26 [1958], Mr. Dukuly addressed the General Assembly of the United Nations and came out for what could be described as almost a neutralist position between the Union of Soviet Socialist Republics and the United States of America. This was put on the front page of *Pravda,* according to the Russian radio broadcast which gave listeners in Liberia their *first* account of what the Liberian Secretary of State had told the United Nations!

Let us not exaggerate Russian relations with Liberia. After the widely publicized Russian visit to Monrovia, and the talk about diplomatic relations. President Tubman and influential Liberians became quite cool to the idea of Russian influence. I doubt whether formalities necessary for the establishment of a USSR Embassy will be completed for some years—if ever.

Liberia wants to be a friend of America. Liberia needs a friend. Perhaps the United States needs Liberia if America is to have other friends in the same social circle. The unchipped green glass beer bottle symbolizes Liberian economic advancement. But it is possible that even more than economic progress Liberia wants warm, international friendships of the kind that could be mutually helpful.

CLASHES SPREAD OVER CAMEROON [11]

A visitor arriving in the Cameroon capital of Yaoundé early yesterday for the new nation's independence celebration was accosted by an official greeter. Upon learning that the guest

[11] From news story by Homer Bigart, New York *Times* correspondent. New York *Times.* p 20. Ja. 3, '60. Reprinted by permission.

was an American, the greeter whispered: "Remember, three of every four Cameroon people are against this government."

This morning at the Douala airport another furtive voice predicted a revolution in "four or five days" would topple the newly independent government.

The atmosphere could properly be called sinister. As home-bound diplomats prepared to board a plane early today shots were heard in the direction of the city. African troops led by French officers ran through the terminal.

Minutes later a wounded youth with hands up was marched past with a machete against his back.

Clashes have occurred almost daily since last June.

The most embarrassing incident occurred . . . [one] night when rebels simultaneously attacked the police headquarters and the airport a few hours before foreign diplomats arrived. Government sources said thirty were killed, but some observers said casualties were more than one hundred and that two French officers were among the dead.

The government attributed the outbreak to the terrorist wing of the outlawed Union of the Cameroon People. Observers cautioned, however, that discontent was so widespread that not every incident could be attributed to that party, regarded by some as Communist-dominated.

The party has ably exploited economic and social unrest in the Bamileké region on the frontier of the British Cameroons. In this overpopulated area the youth of the Bamileké tribe are spreading revolt against their own chiefs, who hold all land and most of the women. Some chiefs are said to have 100 wives.

The youths are rebelling against a feudal society and the concept of national independence has little meaning to them.

The Union of the Cameroon People contends that independence under the country's present Premier, Amadou Ahidjo, only perpetuates French rule. Unfortunately, it does appear that without French military support the Ahidjo regime would hardly expect to survive.

The Cameroon Army exists only on paper. Two companies are being recruited. Two other companies are being formed from soldiers transferred from French units.

Premier Ahidjo is expected to ask the French to help in smashing the spreading revolt.

It was apparent that Cameroon faces a desperate struggle for internal stability. . . .

Cameroon's trouble springs from the fact that she has no ethnic religious or geographic unity. Her densely populated north is dominated by a powerful Moslem ruling class that treats the pagan masses as virtual slaves. The north is fifty years behind the rest of the country in social and educational development.

Premier Ahidjo is a Moslem from the north. His father was a slave. So long as he is supported by the north he seems likely to win national elections that have been promised some time in the next six months. His opposition lacks unity.

The Premier's critics contend his government is unrepresentative. Cameroon does not yet have a constitution and Premier Ahidjo has been governing by decree. . . .

Cameroon, tucked on the remote bend of the Gulf of Guinea, is slightly bigger than California. It has more than 3.25 million people. Its economy is purely agricultural but recently a large bauxite deposit was discovered north of Yaoundé. There are fewer than 17,000 Europeans.

CRUSHING ISSUES FACE CAMEROON [12]

Of all emerging African nations, Cameroon, which achieved independence January 1 [1960], seems least likely to succeed.

An agonizing and desperate dilemma confronts its Premier, Ahmadou Ahidjo. He must either crush a rebellion in the south with ruthless tactics, risking international censure, or treat with the Bamileké rebel leaders and legalize the outlawed Union of Cameroon Peoples, a move that could unseat him in the April elections. . . .

[12] From news story by Homer Bigart, New York *Times* correspondent. New York *Times*. p 4. Ja. 25, '60. Reprinted by permission.

His task is formidable. Most of the Bamileké region lies under the control of the insurgents, who are levying taxes on a majority of the region's population of 550,000. The armed insurgents probably number fewer than 1,000 but they are able to keep the people in line through an odd combination of black magic, Leftist propaganda and terrorism.

The Bamileké are considered to be the cleverest and hardest working of the 400-odd peoples that comprise Cameroon. Their hill region, abounding in coffee and bananas, is most attractive.

Population density reaches 200 to 300 to a square mile. Demographic pressures forced thousands of landless, jobless Bamileké to migrate to the port city of Douala or the capital, Yaoundé. There, where they are hated, feared and discriminated against by lazier folk, the Bamileké become easily susceptible to anti-government agitation.

The Bamileké are only one of the many southern tribes that resent the government, which is dominated by a Moslem who is sincerely trying to weld north and south into one nation. It is feared because his chief supporters are powerful Moslem chiefs ruling as feudal lords over the pagan masses in the north.

Only a sentimentalist would call Cameroon a nation. A mere handful of its 3.25 million citizens have any grasp of the concept of nationhood. The loyalty of the rest is exclusively tribal and regional. During their forty-six-year rule the French did nothing to detribalize the country or otherwise encourage integration.

Like her neighbor Nigeria, Cameroon lies at an ethnic crossroads of Africa and holds a bewildering hodgepodge of races. . . . Unlike British-ruled Nigeria, Cameroon was held by a foreign power that gave little thought to the development of an efficient, dedicated cadre of native officials drawn from different sections of the country. . . .

Formerly the major part of the German colony of Kamerun, the territory was ceded to France under a League of Nations mandate after World War I. This was replaced after World War II by a United Nations trusteeship agreement. Cameroon was given full internal autonomy in 1957 and the United Nations voted last March to grant full independence January 1.

The stage already had been set for civil war. In 1957 the Union of Cameroon Peoples was outlawed by the government, which had Premier Ahidjo as its Interior Minister. The group's leader, Dr. Félix-Roland Moumie, fled the country and is now attempting to control the Bamileké revolt from Conakry, Guinea.

Dr. Moumie, backed by Ghana, Guinea and India, demanded United Nations supervised elections before independence. This M. Ahidjo successfully opposed.

The rebels promise social and economic reforms, including the end of taxation once the war is won, and higher prices for coffee, the region's main cash crop.

M. Djoumessi agreed that not all the rebels were inspired by "Moumie and his gangsters" but that some had legitimate grievances against "bad" local chiefs who imposed heavy taxation.

THE ECONOMY OF THE BELGIAN CONGO [13]

A burst of economic development, the like of which colonial Africa had never seen, is picking up speed now here in the "green hell" of the Belgian Congo.

Undeterred by political unrest among the natives, the Belgians are going ahead with a new ten-year plan for tapping the resources of the colony.

Roads and railways are being pushed into the interior. Bridges are being built over crocodile-infested rivers. Airports are opening up areas that previously were all but inaccessible.

In the steaming interior, plantations are being carved out of the jungle. Mine production is increasing after a long slump. Modern cities are springing up throughout the territory.

If all goes well, construction of a big dam on the Congo River will begin within a few years and may, eventually, become part of the largest hydroelectric development in the world. . . .

The city of Leopoldville, situated 300 miles up the river from the Atlantic Ocean, is becoming one of the biggest cities in colonial Africa. It is the Congo's capital.

[13] From "In the Congo's Jungles, a Boom and a Ferment." *U.S. News & World Report.* 46:92-7+. Ap. 20, '59. Reprinted from *U.S. News & World Report,* an independent weekly news magazine published at Washington. Copyright 1959 United States News Publishing Corporation.

Population now stands at an estimated 21,000 whites and 360,000 black Africans. That's more than eight times the pre-war figure.

As African cities go, Leopoldville is the most modern of them all. There are air-conditioned hotels, luxury shops, restaurants, night clubs and sidewalk cafes. You can buy just about anything you want here—from a Cadillac to a Parisian gown to a thousand-dollar movie camera.

Something of a boom in construction is giving Leopoldville the skyline of an American city. Office buildings of up to sixteen stories are being constructed. A network of divided-lane boulevards has been laid out. A new airport with jet-length runways has just been opened at a cost of $17 million. Leopoldville has a sports stadium that seats 75,000 people.

On a low range of green hills overlooking the city, a new university, called Lovanium, has been founded. Last autumn it graduated its first class—seven black Africans and four whites. In the native quarters of the city, the Belgians are pushing what is considered the biggest and best housing program in Africa. More than twenty thousand model homes and apartments have been built for the natives in recent years at a cost of $40 million. . . .

White people find that the Congo is good to them financially, and brutal as far as the climate is concerned.

During much of the year, the heat and humidity are so intensive that a shirt wilts in a few minutes. Even a moderate amount of work quickly saps your energy. In the high altitudes of the Eastern Congo, the days are somewhat cooler and drier. Yet, even so, there are fewer than ten thousand whites who have settled permanently in the Congo. The rest come to make money, wilt in the tropical climate and dream of the day when they will pack up and leave.

On a tour of the interior of the Congo, your most vivid impression is of vast size and emptiness.

There are a few thriving cities in the hinterland. Stanleyville, a thousand miles up the river from Leopoldville, has become a center for plantation agriculture and for the transshipment of goods on the river. Bukavu, capital of the Kivu province in the

Eastern Congo, is becoming a holiday resort. In the Katanga province in the southeast, three industrial towns, Elisabethville, Jadotville and Kolwezi, have grown up around the Congo's copper mines.

Yet, in flying from one of these cities to another, you find that the jungle quickly closes in a few miles from the end of the airport runways. For hundreds of miles, there is nothing but a rolling blanket of green, broken here and there by the winding pathway of a great river.

There are only a few territories in Africa that are as big as the Congo, and none of them is anywhere near as rich. The Congo covers more than 900,000 square miles of the central part of the continent. That makes it nearly 80 times the size of Belgium, and about a fourth the size of the United States.

In all that vast expanse, there are only 13.2 million Africans and 115,000 whites. In some of the most fertile areas, population density stands at only three or four natives to the square mile.

The Real "Dark Continent"

The Congo, alone among all the territories of Africa, actually resembles the popular notion of what the Dark Continent should look like. It is covered with thick jungles and is literally soaked with water. Torrential downpours are unleashed almost every day.

On a map of the Congo, the rivers stand out like the nerve system of the human body, with the Congo River itself serving as the spinal cord.

The Congo is the fifth-longest river in the world, exceeded only by the Nile, the Mississippi-Missouri, the Amazon and the Yangtze. It rises in the southeastern part of the Congo, near the headwaters of the Nile, then sweeps across the colony in a great arc 2,718 miles long.

In recent years, the government has spent nearly $70 million on river vessels, navigation facilities and dock equipment. Regular service is maintained on the Congo River and fifteen of its tributaries. Together, these total nearly eight thousand miles of waterways.

Because of the presence of the river as a free highway, the Belgians have built only a few long-distance roads and railroads in the colony. Most of the railroads are short-haul lines, used to detour around rapids in the river system.

Along with all of the other new activity in the Belgian Congo, the eastern part of the colony is becoming one of the big attractions of Africa.

Even by African standards, the Eastern Congo is a strange place—with Pygmies, giants, gorillas, snow-covered mountains, live volcanoes and high-altitude lakes.

The Pygmies rank as the greatest curiosity of all. There are about eighty thousand of them in the Congo, survivors of a race that occupied much of this area in prehistoric times. . . .

Now, in an effort to give the Pygmies economic independence and, with it, emancipation from serfdom, the Belgians are providing them with free land and tools. . . .

Fading Color Bar

As part of the "new deal" announced for the Congo's natives, the Belgians are stamping out the last traces of a color bar that has been rapidly disappearing in recent years.

The public schools in Leopoldville were integrated several years ago. Some white parents were bitter about the idea of mixing the races in the classroom, but there was no organized opposition to the move.

For the last couple of years, well-dressed black Africans have been free to patronize Leopoldville's hotels, restaurants and bars. There is an economic barrier—most of them can't afford to pay the astronomical prices that are charged in public places—but the doors are open for those with enough money.

Just this year, the Belgians abolished a color bar in government employment. Previously, a black African was limited to a ceiling of $240 a month after many years of service. That was the starting wage for a Belgian with a high-school education.

Now, there is only one salary scale. Black African officials are free to rise as far as their abilities will take them.

The Belgians now are building what ranks as the first real "welfare state" in Africa.

For example, a common laborer, earning the bare minimum of $20 a month, gets a housing allowance that enables him to rent a two-story home with three bedrooms, electricity, running water, a shower and a toilet. A clerk earning $70 or so a month is able to rent—or buy—a much larger home.

Employers in the Congo are obliged by law to provide their men with either free housing or housing allowances. They have to pay special allowances to men with families. In addition, the employer must furnish free medical care for the employee and his dependents.

Firms with more than a thousand workers must have their own hospitals. Those with fewer employees can contract for medical service, either with the government or with private doctors.

The Congo, too, is one of the few places in Africa where natives have social-security pensions and workmen's-compensation insurance.

Throughout the territory, black Africans hold jobs that in most other parts of the continent would be held by whites or by Asians. Most of the captains of the boats on the Congo River are Africans. The gantry cranes on the river docks are operated entirely by natives. So, too, are railroad trains. Virtually all of the clerks and junior officials in banks and business houses are black Africans.

As the Belgians themselves point out, it isn't a question of altruism on their part, but a matter of saving money. White employees, in most cases, have to be recruited in Belgium. In addition to premium wage, they get costly six-month vacations in Europe each three years. . . .

New Fields for Industry

When it comes to economic development, the Belgians are tackling the job in what also is regarded as a big way.

The Congo is one of the most fabulous territories in Africa. There are minerals from one end of the colony to the other. Its potential in hydroelectric power rates as one of the biggest in the world. The land is highly fertile, yet only a small part of it has ever been cultivated.

The Belgians this year are winding up their first ten-year plan for developing the Congo's resources . . .

It's as if the United States were pumping more than $45 billion a year into public works and related programs.

Private investment, in recent years, has been running at up to $240 million annually.

The Belgians are also investing heavily in river and seaport facilities, health programs, education, housing, public buildings and hydroelectric projects. . . .

The Belgian Congo's agricultural potential is being opened up more and more at this time.

In the steaming jungles of the central part of the colony, bulldozers and gangs of native workmen are clearing land for plantations that will produce palm oil, rubber and other crops. One company alone is investing $6 million a year in its palm-oil holdings.

The potential of the central jungle is rated as immense. It covers more than 270,000 square miles—as big as the six states of Iowa, Illinois, Indiana, Ohio, Kentucky and Tennessee—and less than 2 per cent is under cultivation.

Both companies and individual planters find that it takes capital to open up the jungle. Total investment in clearing the land and waiting for a first crop of rubber come close to $400 per acre. Yet harvests are bountiful, and profits, the planters assure you, are there to be made.

THE POLITICS OF THE BELGIAN CONGO [14]

Until recently Belgium's colonial record in the Congo was favorably regarded by large areas of international opinion. This was partly due to ignorance and to the deliberate smoke-screen

[14] From "Atlantic Report on the World Today—Belgian Congo." *Atlantic Monthly.* 203:4+. Ap. '59.

policy of the authorities on the spot, but it can also be explained by certain peculiarities of the Belgian Congo, which contribute to the country's present political ferment.

Next to the Union of South Africa the Belgian Congo is the most industrialized and urbanized land in Africa. Almost one quarter of the African population is concentrated in urban centers, the percentage rising to as much as 27 and 36 per cent in the provinces of Leopoldville and Elisabethville. Close to 38 per cent of the able-bodied male adults have, willingly or under pressure, left the African economy to work for the Europeans. The exploitation of the country's resources has been pushed with remarkable vigor, and this has given rise to the illusion abroad that the gigantic modification of the Congo landscape which has taken place in the past fifty years has been accomplished by a regime that was concerned with the African's welfare and rights.

Another significant feature of the Congo is the fact that the climate has not encouraged a substantial European settlement except in the province of Kivu and, to a lesser extent, in that of Katanga. There are, in fact, only 110,000 whites in the Congo compared to a Negro population of 13 million. The large companies that have established themselves here have thus, ever since 1930, been forced to develop a skilled labor force and the professional capacities of their Negro employees. The numerical weakness of the whites has been of an unquestionable advantage to the blacks.

By exploiting the country's immense natural resources—for example, the uranium of Katanga—the Belgian colonizers have achieved impressive technical and economic successes which are recognized by the Congolese themselves. The three representatives of the National Congo Movement who attended the Pan African Congress at Accra emphasized their appreciation of these results on a number of occasions, while adding that they were sure that they could put the country's resources to far better use after independence.

Official Belgian propaganda has spread the notion that the Congo's impressive economic and technical development has been accompanied by a corresponding rise in the standard of living of the blacks and in some degree of social justice for them. The January [1959] riots in Leopoldville, which caused the death of at least two hundred Negroes, shattered the image of the smiling black man of the Belgian Congo, grateful to his European benefactor for a full stomach. Yesterday one Negro out of three was unemployed in Leopoldville; today the ratio is one to two.

One of the differences between 1958 and 1959 is that the Belgians now know these things. The colonial authorities, who used to claim that they only tolerated "social" discrimination, now concede the existence of deplorable racial discrimination. It is no longer a secret that the annual income of the black man in the Congo is 2100 Congo francs ($42) and that the income of the European settler is sixty-three times more, or that the Union Minière du Haut Katanga, which employs 50,000 Congolese workers, makes an annual distribution of dividends amounting to some 30 per cent of the total income earned by the 1.2 million African workers of the Congo.

When news of the Leopoldville riots reached Belgium, they were first explained away as a consequence of widespread unemployment and a momentarily defective social situation. But today no one denies that the cause of the tragedy is the political frustration of the Africans. The economic and social conditions prevailing in Leopoldville merely acted to trigger a long-threatening explosion.

The political dissatisfaction of the Congolese is no new phenomenon. To find similar incidents one does not have to go back to the grim abuses during the period of the rubber and ivory trade, which were the targets of the Congo Reform Association at the turn of the century. The chronicle of stern repressions over the past fifteen or twenty years includes the butchery at the Union Minière of 1942, when ninety workers were killed for daring to ask for a salary increase of 50 centimes a day as labor's share of the company's enormous war profits. It includes the killings at Lubuta and Masisi in the Eastern Congo in 1943; the execution of the African policemen who revolted that same year at Luluabourg, the capital of the Kasai; the shootings at Matadi, in the Lower Congo, in 1944.

The common cause of these diverse explosions is this: the stubborn insistence of the Belgian authorities on considering the African of the Congo as infinitely malleable, a kind of work horse who can go on forever with no interest in politics. Shortly after the end of World War II, the Belgian novelist O. P. Gilbert wrote a book entitled *Empire du Silence* in which he said that the black man has two rights: to work and to keep quiet. But the reforms which the author and a few men of progressive views then urged on the Brussels government went unheeded, and the watchword which all of Belgium's political parties adopted was prudence.

It took a Socialist-Liberal government, which came to power in 1954, to destroy the last illusions the Congolese still nourished about the parties of the Belgian capital. Aside from breaking the quasi monopoly which the Catholic missions had on education, this Leftish government simply neglected the Congo. Its colonial minister, M. Buisseret, made an unforgettable name for himself in the Congo by declaring that since the Pygmies had been its first inhabitants, the Bantus had no more right to be in the Congo than the Belgians.

In May of 1956 the Belgian Socialist Party devoted an Extraordinary Congress to the Congo and Ruanda-Urundi and elaborated a sound program for these territories, but this initiative was followed by inertia. The three major Belgian parties, in fact, assumed a common front toward the African colonies, an attitude characterized by a desire to take the problem of the Congo out of politics.

Congolese Political Parties

Meanwhile the first nationalist parties had been forming in the Congo. In 1950 a group of Congolese of Bakongo origin who inhabited Leopoldville founded the Abako, an association of Bakongos. Its original purpose was to favor the mother tongue of the Bakongos, which for half a century had been pushed into the shade in favor of a language spoken by the natives of the Upper Congo regions. But it was not long before these linguistic goals were being replaced by political aims.

The Abako first attracted widespread attention in August of 1956 when it launched a vigorous attack upon another well-known native group called Conscience Africaine. This movement had published a manifesto in May, 1956, which appears to have been inspired by European Catholics of more or less progressive views. The manifesto spoke for the first time of the Congo "nation," but in spite of this Conscience Africaine had indicated a lack of interest in the political liberties of the Congolese and a hostility toward the constitution of native political parties.

The attack on Conscience Africaine touched off a lively controversy, in the course of which the Abako was accused of being a party of revolutionary fanatics interested in provoking interracial conflicts and of harboring international designs aimed at obliterating the existing frontiers of the Congo. These accusations did not, however, halt the now-general drift away from semipolitical groups in Leopoldville which were of European inspiration or membership. "What we want," the new political group, Action Socialiste, declared in January of 1958, "is the creation of native parties, based on a determined policy, be it Socialist, Christian Democratic, or Liberal . . . and on socio-economic doctrines which are capable of being adopted by any people in a country which is industrialized or in a process of industrialization."

To these new appeals and yearnings the Belgian administration turned a deaf ear, even going so far as to ban the African weekly *Congo* in August, 1957. After many hesitations it did, however, consent to the holding of elections in a few towns. But they were organized in such a way as to cut across natural political issues and to split the electorate by reactivating old tribal differences. In the key center of Leopoldville the voters thus coalesced into four associations of a tribal type: the Abako, the Association of the Bangalas, the Kasai Federation, and the Kwango-Kwilu Federation. Nevertheless, the leaders of the Abako, who had sometimes shown a marked hostility toward other ethnic groups, now sought to speak for the entire Congo.

The Leopoldville elections of December, 1957, turned out to be a triumph for the Abako, which had had time to sink deep roots there under the forceful leadership of Kasavubu, the mayor of the Dendale commune.

The results encouraged the aspirations of the Africans, as was made clear in the inaugural speech delivered by Kasavubu in April of 1958, in which he demanded the creation of scholarships for Congolese, the admission of many Congolese boys and girls to European universities, recognition of the Congo's nationhood, freedom of the press, and the institution of a democratic regime.

> There is no democracy here [he declared], since in the police force we do not see Congolese policemen. So too in the militia we never hear of Congolese officers, nor of Congolese directors in the medical corps. And what are we to say about the direction and inspection of the educational system? There is no democracy so long as suffrage is not generalized. The first step has not yet been taken. We demand general elections and internal autonomy.

THE FUTURE OF THE BELGIAN CONGO [15]

[In December 1959], a group of Congolese nationalists had the audacity to confront King Baudouin of the Belgians with demands for "immediate total independence." It was enough to make Baudouin's granduncle, King Leopold II, start spinning in his grave.

Leopold II had a simple and direct approach to Congo and the Congolese. They existed to be exploited. The treatment that accompanied this exploitation was something special. Leopold's agents cut off the hands or feet of Africans who failed to fulfill rubber or ivory quotas.

[15] From "The Belgian Congo—A Case History of Nationalism in Africa," article by Homer Bigart, New York *Times* correspondent. New York *Times News of the Week in Review.* p E4. Ja. 3, '60.

The atrocities were horrible enough to shock international opinion at a time (1908) when tough, free-wheeling colonialism was *de rigueur.*

This horror was immortalized by Vachel Lindsay in "The Congo":

> Listen to the yell of Leopold's ghost
> Burning in Hell for his hand-maimed host.
> Hear how the demons chuckle and yell
> Cutting his hands off, down in Hell.

Baskets of hands, salted and smoked to preserve them in the dank climate, were brought in from the bush by Leopold's labor-gang bosses to prove they were on the job.

The Belgian Congo was forged by Leopold and by Henry M. Stanley who, as reporter for an enterprising but eccentric newspaper, "found" Dr. Livingston and then as Leopold's agent signed treaties with native chiefs that formed the basis of Leopold's claim to that vast empire of the equatorial rain forest.

The Berlin Conference of 1885, which divided Africa among the powers, gave the Congo "Free" state to Leopold outright. For twenty years, Leopold ruled the Congo as his personal property. Then, under pressure of world opinion, Leopold surrendered it to the Belgian Parliament.

It is painful to recall Leopold's grim rule, but useful as illustration of the amazing transformation of the Belgian attitude toward the Congolese in seventy-five short years.

A benign policy was dictated partly by determination to atone for Leopold's sins, but also by a shrewd Belgian belief that African nationalism could be forestalled indefinitely by improving the welfare of the people and by ruling sternly but fairly.

This theory might have worked had it been possible to isolate the Belgian Congo from the virus of freedom that spread rapidly across Africa after World War II.

The Belgians concentrated on economic development and worked a miracle. Belgian imperial policy for generations deprived both the Africans and the European settlers of any political rights whatever. But the immense wealth of the Congo, producing for years more than half the free world's uranium and much of its copper and industrial diamonds, enabled Belgium to support an ambitious social-welfare program.

Modern cities, a network of roads, improved medical services, and at long last a start toward decent housing and schools for the Africans made the Congo seem far ahead of the rest of Africa, including the newly independent states. The whole emphasis was on material welfare. The Belgians kept insisting that the Congolese were not ready for self-rule and needed years of "assimilation."

The literacy rate came to 40 per cent, the highest in sub-Saharan Africa. Africans were trained for skilled jobs. Vocational schools were created even in rural districts, and finally, a few years ago, some professions were opened to Africans.

Only a year ago the complacent whites were congratulating themselves on having avoided the violent unrest and racial tensions of Kenya, the Rhodesias and South Africa. . . .

Thus the Leopoldville rioting [in] January [1959] came as a rude awakening. A sudden spasm of fury shook the Bakongo, the lower Congo people who are the majority tribe in the native city. This tribe, perhaps the most politically advanced of the two hundred tribes in the Congo, had a well-disciplined political organization called Abako led by Joseph Kasavubu, a plump, soft-spoken former accountant who once studied for the priesthood.

The riots occurred against a background of serious urban unemployment, but they were stimulated also by some small political concessions.

The government had taken a first cautious step toward enfranchising the masses. In Leopoldville and other cities, the people were allowed indirectly to choose local councils. Mr. Kasavubu was elected Mayor of one of the thirteen Leopoldville communes.

There was stimulus also in the strange developments across the river, where what had been French Equatorial Africa was now a parcel of autonomous republics.

Meanwhile, the Belgian Congo Government stopped trying to isolate the Congolese from the contagion of freedom. Three political leaders were allowed to attend the Pan African Conference at Accra in October, 1958.

The Belgian government's first reaction to the Leopoldville riots was to tighten security. More than 20,000 jobless Africans were rounded up in a series of *ratisages* (rakings) and sent back to rural homes. Although there was no trace of an organized underground or anything resembling the Mau Mau terrorists of Kenya, the Belgians remained in a high state of jitters. Seeing that control of an area seventy-seven times as big as Belgium would be impossible to maintain in the face of an aroused Congolese population, the Belgian government sensibly decided to yield more self-rule.

The first offer of an increase in local and provincial self-government with eventual independence failed to satisfy the Congolese. Tension continued and, finally, after the Stanleyville riots two months ago, Brussels decided on a dramatic acceleration of steps to full independence.

It was announced that provincial elections would be held in March [1960], followed by the election of a national parliament in late summer or early fall. But the cries for immediate independence were so insistent that a few weeks ago the Belgian government proposed national elections in March, simultaneously with the provincial elections.

This sweeping capitulation has embarrassed the nationalist leaders. . . . Political evolution has been molded by regional rather than national aspirations.

Confronted by the reality of early independence, Mr. Kasavubu, Albert Kalonji, a leader of the National Congolese Movement, the heads of other parties favoring a federal state began a feverish study of govenmental forms. They were like students who had long neglected their homework and were now seized by panic on the eve of a final examination.

When the Belgian Minister for the Congo, Auguste de Schryver, refused to advance the date of the Brussels round-table conference—at which the transfer of sovereign power to the new

Parliament will be discussed—from mid-January to January 5, Messrs. Kasavubu and Kalonji roared loudly for local consumption but were secretly relieved. Mr. Kasavubu admitted unreadiness by remarking that the Congolese were looking for experts to guide them in planning a federalist structure.

Whether the Congolese are ready or not, Belgium seems determined to shed her colonial responsibilities as soon as the transfer of sovereignty can be effected without strife or economic dislocation. Formidable problems confront the new nation. The six provinces are all markedly different, and in at least one—the rich mining province of Katanga—there is a strong separatist feeling. Nowhere except in the urban centers, such as Leopoldville, is there a deep understanding of the Congolese national concept. [At the Brussels round-table conference it was agreed that the Belgian Congo would become independent June 30, 1960, following the national elections, rescheduled for May 1960.—Ed.]

Already in Kasai Province fighting has developed between the Lulua and the Baluba tribes and civil war threatens to spread as soon as the Belgians leave. In this instance, the Lulua fear domination by the hated Baluba when independence comes.

Independence for the Belgian Congo, richest colonial prize in Africa, would surely accelerate the native unrest in the remaining African colonial territories, especially in the adjacent British Federation of Rhodesia and Nyasaland.

It might even shake Portuguese Angola and Mozambique, where the Portuguese secret police so far have been able to stamp out the few sparks of freedom that have appeared.

III. POLITICAL AND ECONOMIC OUTLOOK

EDITOR'S INTRODUCTION

Three leading politico-social problems stand out in West Africa: What is the future of tribalism—has it anything to contribute to the "African personality" for which African leaders are searching or should it be smashed completely? What forms of government can deal with the particular problems of West Africa? Will federation movements reunite an area which is fragmented not only by the original tribal structure but also by the artificial frontiers set up by the European colonizing powers during the nineteenth century?

Articles in the first part of this section discuss these issues. In the first two articles an African leader and an American authority on African affairs discuss democracy, suggesting that an attempt must be made to redefine it so that attention is concentrated not on forms of government but on its content. The third selection treats the prospect for federation.

But Africa's hope for *any* form of stable government rests on her ability to increase her rate of economic growth. The problems she meets in trying to reach this goal are similar to those in other underdeveloped parts of the world. She must try to satisfy the rising demand for better living conditions, to provide for the rapid increase in population, to encourage saving and investment, and to obtain foreign aid where internal resources are inadequate.

The growth of the economies of certain African countries has been fairly rapid in recent years but progress has tended to be concentrated on the exploitation of mineral resources and has not had a great effect on over-all living standards. The article from *Fortune,* "Africa Joins the World," describes past progress and future prospects. The next two selections set forth the progress that has been made in securing cooperation throughout the continent and the last demonstrates the comparative neglect of the needs of Africa by the United States.

KEY QUESTIONS FOR AWAKENING AFRICA [1]

At the invitation of the American Committee on Africa, I recently visited the United States for a six-week lecture tour in an effort to explain the new Africa—its problems and aspirations—to the American people. I spoke in every section of the country, and met people of widely varied interests: congressmen and senators, State Department officials, labor leaders, governors and mayors, college and university students and teachers, newspaper men and broadcasters and Negro leaders. I think, therefore, that my impressions are fairly representative of a cross-section of the American people.

Having visited the United States in 1956, I was much impressed with the increase in knowledge about Africa. The questions I was asked were based more on interested understanding than on detached curiosity. . . . [Certain] questions in particular which seemed to trouble Americans came up at almost every meeting. I should like to answer them here.

(1) *Are Africans ready for self-government?*

I was often reminded of the lack of adequate numbers of educated personnel to run the new governments which we in Africa have been demanding. I was told that the high illiteracy rate in many dependent territories would make it impossible for Africans to operate a democracy successfully.

While conceding that Africa has a long way to go toward creating a generally literate community, I answered that this was a common argument used by colonial powers in defense of their continued rule. Often my questioners assumed that the colonial powers were primarily concerned with the education of our people, and that there were deliberate training programs looking toward the day of independence.

[1] From article by Tom Mboya, member of the Legislative Council of Kenya and chairman of the All African People's Conference. New York *Times Magazine.* p 8+. Je. 28, '59. Reprinted by permission.

In fact, however, colonial systems give priority to—and indeed are based upon—such activities as permit or promote the human and material exploitation of the people and territories concerned. Effort is concentrated on extractive industries and quick profits. In every case, investment in education, public health, and other social development programs lags behind.

Ghana's recent history clearly illustrates what I mean. When the all-African Cabinet took over the government, about 20 per cent of the country's children were in school. In five years, this government has raised the figure to 85 per cent and continues to open a new school every other day. There had been nothing to equal this in eighty years of colonial rule.

In areas with a European settler community the problem is even worse. Not only does African education lag behind, but African political rights are subordinated to European domination. Thus, while France has ultimately conceded freedom for Tunisians and Moroccans, she refuses to recognize that Algerians—a people with similar aspirations, history and background—are entitled to the same status. The British concede the rights of Africans on the West Coast, in Somalia and Uganda—and soon in Tanganyika—but refuse to go all the way in Kenya, and certainly dispute these rights in the Central African Federation of Nyasaland and the Rhodesias.

In Africa, Britain has adopted various formulas of qualitative franchise, not based on any training program for independence, but aimed at preserving the position of the white settlers. Thus, in Uganda, where there is a comparatively small settler community, literacy in the vernacular is the minimum qualification for the vote. But in Kenya, where adult suffrage is granted settlers and Asians, the African franchise is limited by such qualifications as an income of £120 or eight years of education. In Central Africa, in addition to rigid control of the number of Africans allowed in the Parliament, the initial qualification for the vote is a £750 income.

In Portuguese areas there is not even a pretense at development or training for future self-government. The Portuguese maintain that Angola and Mozambique are integral parts of Portugal, and insist that all indigenous people may be assimilated as Portuguese citizens, but less than 1 per cent of the African population has been. Slave labor, forced labor, and brutal treatment of Africans is common. No freedom of assembly, association, or the press exists and schools are rigidly controlled by the state with the apparent sanction of the church.

In these so-called multiracial areas, representation in the legislatures is based on communal divisions—i.e., fourteen elected members for 60,000 Europeans and an equal number for 6 million Africans in Kenya, ten elected members for 20,000 Europeans and an equal number for 8 million Africans in Tanganyika. In Kenya, the per capita expenditure on the education of a European child amounts to £32 a year, while that for an African child is £5.

This, then, is my answer to those who ask us to wait until we are prepared by the colonial powers for self-government. While we are appreciative of the benefits we have derived from our contacts with Europe and other parts of the world—especially in the postwar period—we are convinced that if we are to develop rapidly and effectively, as indeed we must if we are to meet the technological and scientific challenges of the twentieth century, we must not only have an effective voice in the government of our countries, but become masters of our own fate. To suggest that this would lead to an overnight reversion to barbarity shows an utter disregard for history and the fact that Africa, despite her many temporary handicaps, lives in the twentieth century, receptive to all the influences of the attitudes and developments of the present.

The question is not whether African freedom will come, but how and when. Even in areas where there is white settlement it must come, and it is futile to think otherwise. In this context, all one can say about South Africa is that her prospects look blacker each year.

(2) Is the African independence movement democratic?

African nations, like all others, enjoy the right to experiment, and above all the right to make mistakes. It is true that a lot depends on the personality of the leadership, especially during the early days of independence. There does not seem to be, however, any alternative to this period of youth and adventure. To think that continued colonial rule would offer a solution is not only to be unrealistic but to indulge in the highest degree of wishful thinking.

If honest mistakes are made we should not be apologetic, for this is part of the process of operating a democracy the world over. It is ironic—and, indeed, flattering—that the older powers should ask us to guarantee perfection when they have not, even after hundreds of years, reached perfection themselves.

Some non-Africans are concerned about the development of opposition parties and others about the forms that governmental institutions will take. Many people seem to expect that Africa must keep what she inherits from her former colonial masters. Africa cannot, however, for very obvious reasons, adopt a blueprint of European or American institutions. Her governmental institutions must recognize Africa's cultural and social background and must move away from the forms used by the colonial powers—fitted for indirect rule—to a representative system.

Opposition parties are a desirable and healthy development, but they must not merely point accusing fingers at the party in power when difficulties arise. Both sides must play the game according to certain rules.

It is unrealistic to expect effective opposition parties in the early days of independence, when the momentum and personality of the liberation movement is still strong and popular, and when genuine differences are usually lacking. To suggest that the popular leaders who combine during the struggle for liberation should break up and form different parties because the book so requires is not only reckless but is to ignore the urgent problems that a new state faces. The solution to these problems requires a stable government that can also offer security for expanded economic growth. The responsibility thrust on the shoulders of both the party in power and the often weak, ineffective opposition party is tremendous and one which requires strength of character, honesty of purpose and, above all, a deep conviction in the service of the country and the people.

IS DEMOCRACY POSSIBLE IN AFRICA? [2]

Critics of Africa's new governments, which have displayed dictatorial characteristics, often argue that self-rule should be withheld until democracy can be assured in Africa. Desirable as this would be, it is difficult to see how a colonial power could insist on withholding independence until a people had demonstrated its capacity to operate democratically. For colonial rule, by its very nature, is a contradiction of democracy, and even with the best of intentions a technologically backward non-Western country cannot begin to develop on democratic lines until it has ceased to be subject to colonial authority. Nor can the Western nations, when they look back on the political institutions they had established at the same stage of economic growth as Ghana or Guinea, truthfully claim that twentieth century democracy was flourishing in England or France in the premedieval period, or even by 1900.

Many of Africa's new political leaders—e.g. in Ghana—are first-generation literates, who are proud of having spanned the gulf between their tribal illiterate society and the responsible posts they occupy as administrators and diplomats, but have not had an opportunity to acquire the experience in public affairs which Western democracies have accumulated over centuries. Nor does time, in a period of jet-speed changes, permit them to develop new institutions at leisure. The process of political telescoping, characteristic of many non-Western nations, is particularly visible in Africa. Tribal chiefs who resist change are being shorn of authority by modern-minded politicians, who, before they have had time to develop into nineteenth century liberals on the Western model, find themselves already being crowded off the stage by trade-union leaders like Sékou Touré and Tom Mboya. [See "Guinea Outside The French Community" in Section II, above, and preceding article in this section.]

Moreover, the tasks of economic development, on which the colonial powers had made a successful start, but a start largely limited to their own commercial and security needs—such as

[2] Article by Vera M. Dean, author of many books about the non-Western countries. *Foreign Policy Bulletin.* 39:22-4. O. 15, '59. Reprinted by permission.

ports, railways and roads which service European-owned plantations, farms and mines—require intervention by governments for many years to come, as Professor W. W. Rostow of the Massachusetts Institute of Technology has pointed out in his study on economic growth. It is the state, not individual entrepreneurs, foreign or domestic, which will have to build the infrastructure —roads, bridges, dams, additional railways—that will be needed before a soundly-based program for a country's economic "take-off" toward maturity can be effectively started with internal and/or foreign financial resources.

One Man, One Party

Under these circumstances, regrettable as it may seem to those who had hoped independence would automatically bring about democracy, the African states may be expected, at least in the early stages, to live under one-man or one-party rule. This has been made clear by the experience, to date, of African countries with a wide variety of colonial backgrounds. [See articles in Section II, above.] Liberia with William V. S. Tubman, Guinea with Sékou Touré, Ghana with Nkrumah, Tunisia with Habib Bourguiba, the Ivory Coast with Houphouet-Boigny, much as they differ in historical development, religions and cultural heritage they have created out of their own experience or out of the contributions of foreign cultures, have one common denominator. Each is ruled by an able and successful leader who, subject to a few qualifications, is in effect an authoritarian head of state, even though not a totalitarian ruler on the Communist model; and each, when questioned about the existence of an opposition, usually refers to dissenters as "young hotheads" or as "malcontents without a following."

Each has had to use pressures of all kinds, implicitly or explicity, to reduce the power of the tribal chiefs—traditional hereditary or elected rulers—on whom the colonial governments had usually relied to carry out their commands in "the bush." Sékou Touré, with his experience as a trade-union organizer, built a network of local units across Guinea, through which he succeeded in isolating and circumventing the chiefs by peaceful means. Nkrumah, less well prepared for the resistance of the Ashanti chiefs, who rightly feared that the new independent government would end their domination, resorted to strong-arm methods, with the result that dangerous tensions between the new and the old order threatened Ghana from the outset. Experience, however, brought an easing of tensions in 1959, and unless fresh difficulties flare up, Nkrumah may succeed in integrating the old chiefs into a modern state. Thus gradually, throughout Africa, the transfer of power from the *ancien régime* of tribal institutions to twentieth century government, which in other areas of the world involved bloody conflicts, is being effected by relatively peaceful means under the direction of more or less authoritarian politicians.

Nigeria an Exception?

Nigeria, which is slated to achieve independence in October 1960, may prove an exception to this one-man, one-party trend because of three important factors: (1) the need to create, within the Nigerian federation, a balance between the country's three regions with their three main tribal groups—the Yorubas of the western region, led by Chief Obafemi Awolowo, head of the Action party; the Ibos of the eastern region, led by Nnamdi Azikiwe, head of the National Council of Nigeria and the Cameroons (NCNCC); and the Moslems of the northern region, the Hausa and Fulani, whose premier is Sir Alhaji Ahmadu; (2) the democratic ideas and experience of the Yoruba tribe of the western region, whose capital, Ibadan, the most populous city in Africa, is the seat of Nigeria's university; and (3) the newly emerging desire of the Moslems for education and for social reforms, and their respect for British methods of administration. The present prime minister of the federation, Tafawa Balewa, a northerner, is noted for his moderation, his dedication to public service and his gift as reconciler of conflicting factions in Lagos, which is to be the federal capital. The Nigerians have also proved more skillful than other Africans in integrating traditional chiefs into the framework of their emerging parliamentary government through the creation of a House of Chiefs. This house, it is hoped, will give the country the benefit of the views of its elder statesmen who, in turn, will have the satisfaction of participating in the new state's affairs. [For further details see "The Politics of Nigeria" in Section II, above.]

Most of the African political leaders, irrespective of their origins and training, were at one time or another exposed to Communist ideas and influence—whether in the United States, Paris, or London. This was true of Nkrumah, son of a goldsmith, who studied at Lincoln University, Pennsylvania, and in London, and plied many trades to earn a living in the United States; of Sékou Touré—grandson of the famous chief Samory, foe of the French—who did not finish secondary school in Guinea but successfully organized a trade union in the railway administration where he worked, and went on to become a labor leader and in 1956 a member of the French Chamber of Deputies before the creation of the Community; of Houphouet-Boigny, a Catholic, a prosperous physician and planter, now prime minister of the Ivory Coast; and of Tom Mboya, who rose from sanitary inspector in the service of Nairobi's City Council to be general secretary of the Kenya Federation of Labor and leader of the Independence Movement party formed in August 1959, and hopes to be Kenya's first prime minister.

Nor was this widespread interest in communism either fortuitous or surprising. For in the depression years of the 1930's and again after World War II, when the Communists, particularly in France exercised a significant influence, communism seemed the most promising ally of those who were seeking independence from colonial rule in Africa. This does not mean, however, that African leaders became either blind followers or tools of communism, as their political opponents often assert. Their passionate desire for independence means independence from Communist intervention as well as from Western colonialism—as Nkrumah proved when he turned to Israel, not to the U.S.S.R., for economic aid as complement to the aid received from Britain.

Other African leaders, trained for the priesthood in Catholic seminaries, which at one time offered the best opportunity for higher education, but later abandoned their vocation—notably

Abbé Fulbert Youlou, premier of the Congo Republic and the late Barthélemy Boganda, the able premier of the Central African Republic, killed in an airplane accident in 1959—even if not suspected of past Communist sympathies, have shared some of the social ideas of their Marxist-inspired contemporaries.

The real test of the intentions of the African leaders will be not their predilection for or opposition to communism, but the direction they take on two major issues: (1) racialism—will they seek an Africa for Africans, to the exclusion of Europeans and Asians?; and (2) orientation in world affairs—will they retain links with the French Community, the British Commonwealth, a Belgian-Congolese Community of the future, or drift into the Soviet orbit, or adopt a policy of neutralism?

MOVEMENTS FOR A UNITED AFRICA [3]

It is not chance that the phrase "the balkanization of Africa" was first used by Africans in French territory. The same centralization of authority which marked French colonial control, and which has tended to reduce the force of tribalism in her former territories, accustomed the African peoples there to think in terms of larger independent political units. Among English-speaking Africans the impulse for a "United Africa" came from various sources, including the United States, where certain leading African nationalists studied. Thinking along these lines has also responded to a doctrine of some economists that a small state is less viable than a large one, examples to the contrary, ranging from Costa Rica to Denmark and Switzerland, notwithstanding.

The first legal action to implement African unity was the Ghana-Guinea agreement of November 28, 1958. Initially termed a "union," it has thus far taken the shape of an alliance. Its status was further clarified in May 1959, when the leaders of the two countries met and discussed common problems. It was, first of all, to be the nucleus of a larger grouping, to which all other

[3] From *United States Foreign Policy: Africa; A Study,* prepared at the request of the Senate Committee on Foreign Relations, by Northwestern University Program of African Studies. United States. Senate. Committee on Foreign Relations. 86th Congress, 1st session. Supt. of Docs. Washington 25, D.C. '59. p 27-9.

African states would be invited to adhere, with each member state or federation preserving its own personality and its own internal structure. Each would have its own diplomatic representation, and individuals would have double citizenship. Each adhering country would have its own army, but there would be a common defense policy; the Union's flag would be red, yellow, and green, with a black star for each member state. Said M. Sékou Touré: "We have chosen independence, not for the profit of Guinea but for that of Africa." Said Mr. Nkrumah: "We thought at first of a United States of West Africa, but events have gone so fast that we are now thinking about the unity of all Africa."

At the July meeting of the Presidents of Liberia and Guinea and the Prime Minister of Ghana, the question of African unity was faced in a somewhat different manner. Here President Tubman was able to bring his colleagues to his position that while some form of association between African states is desirable, it should for the time being remain looser than the concept of "Union" implies. These three leaders, deferring action because of the impending independence of other African territories, called for the creation of a community of independent African states. This is to be discussed at a special conference to be held in 1960 of independent African states and "nonindependent states that have fixed dates on which they will achieve independence."

In April 1958, the first Conference of Independent African States was held in Accra. This conference reaffirmed an All African anticolonialist stand and, including as it did the North African states and Liberia, laid the foundation for a formally constituted African Caucusing Group in the United Nations. In December the All African People's Conference met; it was much more broadly based and essentially sub-Saharan in its attendance and orientation. Early in 1959, it was reported that Senegal, Soudan, Upper Volta, and Dahomey would constitute a federation within the French Community, but in its final form, under the name of Mali, it included only the first two. The other two joined the remaining autonomous republics, excepting Mauritania, in forming a customs union, led by the Ivory Coast, with which Mali became associated at a meeting held in June. In former French Equatorial Africa there are both separatist and unifying tendencies; a customs union has been formed of the four autonomous republics, but no closer association seems likely at the present time. An East African Federation is improbable as long as the role of the European settler community in Kenya remains unresolved. The future of the Federation of the Rhodesias and Nyasaland is uncertain.

Northern and Sub-Saharan Africa

Pan Africanism, as it has developed since the doctrine was enunciated at the end of the First World War, essentially concerned sub-Saharan Africa. North Africa entered lightly, if at all; in its earlier forms, it might even be said that it was a West African concept and movement, inspired by American Negroes, and had much stronger roots in British than in French territories. The first Pan African Congress was convened in Paris in 1918-1919, another in Lisbon in 1923, and a third in New York City in 1927. More fully African in representation and more sophisticated in tactical competence was the Pan African Nationalist Congress held in Manchester in 1945, whose membership included Kwame Nkrumah, his late political adviser, George Padmore, and Jomo Kenyatta.

North Africa has come into this picture only recently. The distinction between North and sub-Saharan Africa rests on certain evidence of scholarship of an historical, cultural, religious, ethnic, and linguistic nature. There has, however, been centuries-long trade across the desert, with the societies of the Berber and Arab north and the Negro south effecting the cultural and biological interchanges of all peoples in contact. Islam spread well below the Sahara; something more than 22 per cent of the sub-Saharan population are Moslems, with the same proportion professing Christianity and about 55 per cent holding to their aboriginal religions.

President Nasser's book, *Egypt's Liberation,* is one of the few available expressions of North African thinking about relations with the countries to the south. The brevity with which sub-Saharan Africa is treated, and the attitude toward its peoples and cultures reflected in it, are revealing. In the two-page section dealing with it, headed "The Interior of the Dark Continent," President Nasser tells us: "I will continue to dream of the day when I will find in Cairo a great African institute dedicated to unveiling to our view the dark reaches of the continent." He notes how "the peoples of Africa will continue to look to us, who guard their northern gate, and who constitute their link with the outside world."

In words reminiscent of the formulas of the civilizing mission and the white man's burden, he declares that it is "our responsibility to support, with all our might, the spread of enlightenment and civilization to the remotest depths of the jungle," a statement that takes on added significance in view of the explanation, in the preface, that the writer's thoughts were set down "to discover . . . what our role is to be in the succeeding stages of Egypt's history."

The bond which at the present time unites the states of the African continent is clearly one of anticolonialist sentiment. All the members of the African Caucusing Group in the United Nations, except Liberia and Ethiopia, have but recently emerged from tutelage; and Ethiopia, it will be recalled, had this status under Italian domination, from which she was released only at the end of World War II. A common adversary is a powerful unifying force. As one writer on the Conference of African States put it: "what emerged clearly . . . was that some Arab states had more in common with some of the African states than they had with some of their fellow Arab states."

On the other hand, in the light of the attitudes reflected in President Nasser's comments, the fact that the end of 1960 will see the North African states a minority in the United Nations African Caucusing Group and the Conference of African States may be important, especially since it appears that both Ghana and the United Arab Republic aspire to leadership.

AFRICA JOINS THE WORLD [4]

The young African giant is on the move. . . . Most of the continent has been participating handsomely in the unprecedented prosperity and growth enjoyed by the free world during the past decade. At the same time, Africa's nationalism has been rising faster even than its output. At World War II's end some 20 per cent of Africa's population in four countries were to all intents operating on their own. Today more than a third of the people on the continent—in the Union of South Africa, Egypt, Libya, Liberia, Morocco, Ethiopia, Ghana, Tunisia, and the Sudan—can be regarded as self-governing. And within a few years another 40 million Africans are scheduled to achieve independence.

Most of the new countries are run by Africans, and most are aggressively independent. Most also seem beguiled by a proposition that has ensnared more sophisticated people than they: the notion that the alternative to anything imperfect is necessarily something perfect. Because many blame colonialism for all their troubles, real and imaginary, they now expect these problems to be solved forthwith. And because many identified colonialism with private enterprise and international trade, these incline to the notion that the swift and easy way to elevate their living standards lies in government controls over prices and wages, grandiose attempts at economic self-sufficiency, and even socialism.

Nothing would serve rising Africa better than to stop and reconsider objectively its colonial heritage. For whatever colonialism's past political and social shortcomings, it brought to Africa not only development money but an economic libertarianism that was perhaps the best thing that could have happened to the continent. Colonialism brought to Africa (even if it did not always practice them) the free-market principles that enabled Europe and North America, which were underdeveloped lands not so long ago, to develop in the first place. Nor do the new

[4] From article by Curtis Prendergast, bureau chief of *Time*, Johannesburg, at the time the article was written. *Fortune*. 57:124-6. Mr. '58. Courtesy *Fortune*. Copyright 1958 by Time Inc.

African nations have to go far for examples of how to grow. All they have to do is to look around them at the unprecedented progress Africa itself has made in the past decade. . . .

The continent's population, since 1950, has been increasing at 1.7 per cent a year, the same rate at which the U.S. population is growing. But Africa's gross product in the same years has been increasing by an astonishing average of 5 per cent a year, a rate surpassed by no continent and by few countries. To put it another way, Africa's per capita production is increasing by more than 3 per cent a year. Computed at going exchange rates, the continent's gross product or G.N.P. now comes to $28 billion or so. But purchasing power in Africa is much higher than the exchange rate suggests, and *Fortune* estimates that the continent's gross product, figured in U.S. prices, amounts to more than $50 billion (G.N.P. of the U.S. in 1957: $434 billion). So although African gross product is only a small fraction of U.S. gross product, it is growing considerably faster.

And what has been responsible for this remarkable expansion? A major factor has been years of heavy capital investment, most of it by foreign companies and governments, but some of it by Africans themselves. Owing to huge mineral development, capital investment in the Belgian Congo and the Federation of Rhodesia and Nyasaland has been running between 26 per cent and 31 per cent of gross product, a colossal rate; and it has been running at nearly 25 per cent in the Union of South Africa, which accounts for some 22 per cent of Africa's gross product.

Just how much investment amounts to for Africa as a whole is hard to say precisely. Much of the capital invested by small landholders in countries like Ghana and Nigeria never gets into the statistics; but on the other hand there are few African territories or countries in which small landholders are as important as they are in Nigeria and Ghana, where British policy has encouraged them and forbidden the alienation of land for European-owned plantations. . . . Africa is importing some $1.7 billion in capital goods a year. Since capital-goods imports probably amount to between 40 per cent and a half of most African countries' total capital expenditures, the total for the continent probably ranges between $4 billion and $5 billion a year. This works out to between 15 and 20 per cent of the continent's gross product, or above the current average for most of the Western world.

Minerals

Agriculture, of course, always has been and still is Africa's biggest economic activity. But by all odds the most important element in both the continent's recent rate of capital investment and its over-all growth is mining. In the past decade the physical volume of African mineral production has risen more than 60 per cent, and dollar volume has more than tripled, to around $2 billion. In 1956, mineral exports were $1.9 billion, accounting for 34 per cent of the value of all Africa's exports, or double their share in 1948. What is more, mining has stimulated enormously the development of railroads, roads, light manufacturing, service industries, and great power projects.

Africa mines nearly two-thirds of the free world's gold—more than 500 metric tons annually, worth $650 million (most of it in the Union of South Africa). It produces practically all the free world's diamonds, for both jewelry and industrial use, worth a grand total of more than $75 million annually. In 1955 the Belgian Congo alone mined, by weight, 60 per cent of the world's diamonds, but most of them were industrial stones. The Union of South Africa and Ghana together produce less than half the volume of diamonds of the Belgian Congo, but about 20 per cent of Ghana's and 35 per cent of South Africa's are gem diamonds.

More important than either gold or diamond output, because it is growing faster, is copper production, which rose from something over 400,000 metric tons in 1948 to more than 625,000 tons worth $550 million in 1955. By far the biggest African producer is Northern Rhodesia, whose output rose from 217,000 tons in 1948 to 385,000 tons in 1954, fell back to 348,000 tons in 1955, and rose again to 385,000 tons in 1956. But declining copper prices . . . have slowed down the extraordinary expansion enjoyed recently by the Federation of Rhodesia and Nyasaland.

Increasing swiftly is the continent's production of other important metals:

Uranium figures are secret, but the Union of South Africa alone is probably producing about 6,000 tons a year worth upwards of $100 million, and the Belgian Congo may be doing as well.

Lead production, two-thirds of it in Southwest Africa, has soared from 89,000 metric tons in 1948 to 328,000 tons worth $100 million in 1955, a sixth of free world output.

Chrome production in the Union of South Africa and Rhodesia amounts to 436,000 metric tons, about a third of world output.

Cobalt-ore output, most of it in the Belgian Congo, has risen from about 5,000 metric tons in 1948 to some 10,000 metric tons, 70 per cent of world production.

Antimony production, mostly in the Union of South Africa, has risen from 5,700 metric tons in 1948 to some 16,000 tons, nearly half the world output.

Bauxite production in Ghana is about 140,000 metric tons a year; in French West Africa, which produced none a few years ago, it is now 450,000 tons and increasing.

Africa produces 14 per cent of the world's tin, 39 per cent of its manganese, 35 per cent of its phosphates. And iron-ore and coal production, mostly for local use, is growing fast.

And finally there is oil, whose bounty promises to be enormous. Algeria, recently producing almost 600,000 barrels a year, will doubtless increase output spectacularly. Nigeria . . . is showing considerable promise, as is French Equatorial Africa.

Power

Owing largely to modern mining's enormous demands for power, there are now under way or being projected a dozen or more hydroelectric schemes, all of which will produce more power than the mines need. Some of them:

The $240-million Kariba Dam in the Federation of Rhodesia and Nyasaland. . . .

The $45-million Edea aluminum project in the French Cameroons. . . .

The $73-million Owen Falls (Nile River) scheme, designed to supply power for copper mines and industry, among other things, in Uganda, was started in 1950 and by 1960 will have capacity of 150,000 kilowatts. Plans are under way for a second project farther down the river.

The De la Commune and Le Marinel projects on the Upper Congo (the latter is already operating) will have installed capacity of 398,000 kilowatts.

The $150-million Kouilou project near Pointe-Noire in the Middle Congo province of French Equatorial Africa, still in the planning stages, may rival Kariba.

The Konkouré project in French West Africa, also still being planned, is designed to convert French Guinea bauxite into aluminum, calls for the construction of a dam, power station, and a city complete with transportation facilities.

The Cambambe project in Angola and the Chicamba project in Mozambique.

The much-publicized $700-million Volta River scheme, designed to make aluminum from the abundant bauxite deposits in the Volta River basin in Ghana.

And finally, what could be the world's greatest hydroelectric project, the huge Inga scheme, which would use the vast flow of the Congo River to develop mineral and other resources in mid-Africa. One plan calls for eventual installed capacity of 20 million to 25 million kilowatts, three times the present installed capacity of France, and a fifth of the present installed capacity in the U.S. This would cost, over some thirty years, between $3 billion and $4 billion.

Leaving aside Inga and Volta, and making allowance for the fact that world aluminum production is temporarily overexpanded, these projects will soon add some three million or four million kilowatts to the continent's present installed capacity of about six million kilowatts. Since most of the present capacity is in the Union of South Africa, the new plants will obviously multiply severalfold electric power elsewhere.

Industrial Prime Mover

Thus mining, far from merely exhausting the resources of underdeveloped countries (as it is often described as doing), is acting as a kind of prime mover in the continent's development. Considerable power from the hydro developments is always left over for local consumption. Mining payrolls, local purchases, and tax and royalty payments provide the markets and money for commerce, improved agricultural production, and heavy industries like cement, steel, bricks, and construction, to say nothing of secondary consumer industries like soap, beer, shoes, textiles, clothing, and so on. There is no more dramatic example of how this kind of development nourishes itself, once given a good start, than the Federation of Rhodesia and Nyasaland. . . .

At its present rate of growth, and barring a runaway population increase, African purchasing power should be supporting, within a generation, a varied consumer economy. Today about two-thirds of all African consumer expenditures go for food; in another generation more than half may go for goods. What with population increase, the goods market might triple. In the Federation of Rhodesia and Nyasaland, indeed, four African entrepreneurs have already opened a large supermarket called Machipisa Stores Ltd. (*machipisa* means cheap in the local dialect).

The progress of the continent as a whole is revealed in the distribution of the labor force. As yet, only about a quarter of the total African population lives in cities (against 64 per cent in the U.S.); and 63 per cent of the total African labor force, estimated at 72 million, is engaged in agriculture, forestry, and fishing. But the point is that already 10 per cent of the African labor force is employed in transportation, communications, and commerce, 13 per cent in services, 8 per cent in manufacturing, 3 per cent in mining, and 3 per cent in construction. Trend figures for the continent are lacking, but the trend is demonstrated by labor distribution in the more advanced countries. No less than 46 per cent of the working force of Northern and Southern Rhodesia is employed in mining, manufacturing, construction, commerce, transportation, and communication. On the other hand, only 25 per cent of Egypt's working population is working in them, and only 15 per cent of Algeria's.

More to Eat

As wage and income levels rise, of course, the demand for food rises. Thus Africa's agricultural production has risen some 55 per cent since prewar days, while population has risen only 30 per cent. Some of this production, to be sure, is exported, and traditional export crops have on the whole done well. Africa produces about 25 per cent of the world's peanuts (most of them in Nigeria and French West Africa), and their production has risen 60 per cent since 1938. Other African export crops like palm oil (80 per cent of world production) and cocoa (more than 60 per cent of world production) have been rising somewhat. Algerian wine production, reduced by vineyard destruction during the war, is now a third again as large as that of the whole United States. A few exports, such as maize from the Union of South Africa and tobacco from the Federation of Rhodesia and Nyasaland, have soared.

But the most impressive gains, because they reflect the continent's higher standards of living, have been made by products consumed at home—rice, cassava, yams, etc.

The continent's future, like its present, depends largely on foreign capital investment. The great bulk of that investment, more than $1 billion a year (not counting large reinvestments of profits by foreign companies), has been coming from private sources, mostly European. To this must be added more than a billion a year, mostly raised at home, spent by local governments on public works. Both public and private enterprises have received loans from semi-government agencies abroad. Since World War II, for example, the World Bank has lent $432 million for African development—$160 million in the Union of South Africa, $122 million in the Rhodesias, $80 million in the Belgian Congo. The British Colonial Development Corporation has lent a total of $133 million. And in recent years outright grants, mostly from France and Britain and some from the U.S., have totaled at least $250 million a year.

African development is getting more attention than ever from abroad. The common-market countries have already agreed to pump about $1 billion, much of it from West Germany, into French Africa. The Communist-minded Asian-African conference in Cairo . . . [in] January [1958] which seemed designed to discourage private investment in underdeveloped countries, may have the dubious effect of gratuitously stepping up Western government aid. So may the Soviet policy of increasing loans to underdeveloped countries. (The Soviet Union has already committed $465 million to Egypt.) On January 15 [1958], Britain, France, Belgium, and Portugal joined Liberia, Ghana, South Africa, and the Federation of Rhodesia and Nyasaland in setting up a technical assistance plan for Africa south of the Sahara.

Africa, in other words, will probably get a lot of capital. It may even get too much too quickly. The newly independent countries in particular may be tempted to throw away what is their best inheritance from colonialism—namely, reliance on trade, and on private saving and investment—in favor of self-defeating schemes of national sufficiency and rigid government planning. They may try to industrialize too fast with schemes tending to impoverish rather than to improve. But whatever happens, the African market, over the long run, is bound to expand as it never has before.

ECONOMIC COOPERATION [5]

The economies of African states have existed too long as separate, self-contained, isolated entities. African countries have far too long been forced to nurse their own economies and puzzle out their complicated problems by themselves, or else have them handled haphazardly for them by others. We are only too well acquainted with the difficulties and

[5] From "New Era of Economic Cooperation Opens in Africa." *United Nations Review*. 5:5-10. F. '59.

barriers that the African peoples have had to overcome in coming together to deliberate on matters of common interest. But it is impossible to believe that individual countries, working alone and isolated from their neighbors, can ever achieve their objectives, and the African peoples must therefore work and cooperate together if the economic development of this continent is to be furthered.

The words were spoken by His Imperial Majesty Haile Selassie the First, Emperor of Ethiopia, at the inaugural ceremony of the Economic Commission for Africa, newest of the United Nations regional economic commissions, which held its first session in Addis Ababa, Ethiopia, from December 29 [1958] to January 6 [1959]. The words summed up a situation which it is the main task of the new Commission to remedy. According to its terms of reference, the Commission is to initiate and participate in measures for facilitating concerted action for Africa's economic development, including social aspects of such development, with a view to raising the level of economic activity and standards of living in Africa, and for maintaining and strengthening economic relations of African countries and territories both among themselves and with other parts of the world.

Attending the historic session were representatives of countries members of the Commission (Belgium, Ethiopia, France, Ghana, Guinea, Italy, Liberia, Libya, Morocco, Portugal, Spain, Sudan, Tunisia, the United Arab Republic and the United Kingdom) and the representatives of associate members of the Commission (Federation of Nigeria, Kenya and Zanzibar, Trust Territory of Somaliland under Italian administration, Somaliland Protectorate, Tanganyika and Uganda). Also present in a consultative capacity and at their own request were observers from Austria, Brazil, Bulgaria, China, Czechoslovakia, Greece, Hungary, India, Israel, Japan, the Netherlands, Pakistan, Poland, Turkey, the U.S.S.R. the United States and Yugoslavia. In addition, the specialized agencies of the United Nations were represented, as well as a number of non-governmental organizations. One member of the Commission, the Union of South Africa, was unrepresented, as its government had announced that for the present it will not participate in the Commission's work. . . .

In his inaugural address His Imperial Majesty referred to the political "coming of age" of the African peoples as one of the most striking evolutions in the recorded history of mankind. However, he emphasized, political independence was but one part of the complex problems which faced the African peoples in their struggles to achieve their rightful place in the world. He drew special attention to the lag in Africa's economic development and the poverty and hard life of the African peoples, which all could be traced to lack of capital, lack of education and a shortage of technically qualified personnel. Yet Africa was potentially rich and had enormous resources, with the total extent of its wealth not yet known. He felt that the task of the Commission, that of improving the economic condition of all African peoples, was immense. Much labor and toil, he said, would be demanded, not only from the Commission's secretariat, but also from the governments of all countries and territories in fulfilling the commitments and discharging the responsibilities resting upon them.

His Imperial Majesty hoped that the Commission would give serious consideration to finding ways and means of extending immediate economic assistance not only to the independent African countries, but also to the territories on the verge of statehood, since their needs were the most pressing. He outlined certain important matters to which, he said, the Commission should direct its attention, in the fields of trade, statistics, agriculture, public health, transport and communications, as well as measures for the promotion, stabilization and diversification of exports.

Concluding, His Imperial Majesty stated that it was appropriate that the gathering was held under the sponsorship of the United Nations, which was a living and tangible testimonial to the value of cooperative efforts among all men to improve their way of life and to preserve peace. The essential prerequisite for economic and social contentment, he said, was world peace. He prayed that "peace may be vouchsafed to all men, and that the labors of this Commission may ever be conducted in an atmosphere of harmony and cooperation."

UNITED NATIONS SURVEY [6]

African exploration has been extensive for decades, but localized. Now the so-called Dark Continent is to be blanketed by an army of explorers of a different type, dedicated to banishing much of its mystery.

For the next five years, . . . statisticians will be roving its mountains, plains and jungles, reducing to reliable figures every aspect of life in most of the countries and territories. The program is the first major project of the Economic Commission for Africa, which became operative early this year.

Its objective is to establish factual bases for the future economic, financial, and social development of the member nations. The findings are expected to be of immense help to governments in defining their most important problems of food production, provision of adequate financing, discovering domestic resources for capital, and their potentials for trade, among other things. They are also certain to be watched by present and potential investors in the region, some of whom in the past have spent large sums to collect data needed for their specific purposes.

Plans for the survey were approved at the first conference of African statisticians, held early in October [1959] in Addis Ababa, headquarters of the Economic Commission for Africa.

Endorsement of the project by the representatives of nineteen members and associate members is tantamount to ratification. The program will be submitted to the annual meeting of the commission at Tangier in January.

Implementation will follow quickly thereafter, it was indicated. Priorities for the fields of survey will be set by each country. Financing will be primarily the responsibility of the member nations. The United Nations and its agencies will pro-

[6] From "U.N. Survey to Banish Much of Africa's Mystery," news story by Kathleen McLaughlin, New York *Times* correspondent. New York *Times*. p 47. N. 2, '59. Reprinted by permission.

vide many of the statisticians, as well as some of the jeeps in which the teams will travel, and a part of the electrical computing machines to be used for tabulations at the Addis Ababa headquarters.

Among the major features of the prospective survey, one of the most important will be that of population, since a number of the countries have never yet determined their total populations. Lack of adequate figures in this field, including the rates of increase, of deaths and of migrations, has been an obstacle to intelligent planning for future requirements for food, housing, roads, employment, or land use.

In the industry sector of the program, the results will enumerate the number of establishments—at first only the larger ones—classified by type of economic activity, size of plant and number of workers. They will also reckon the capacity of installed power equipment, the value of principal products and of raw materials, gross capital formation, and similar categories.

By consensus of the conference, agriculture constitutes one of the most fertile fields for investigation. Attention will be concentrated on determining the scope of production and the areas of the principal crops, of plantations and other large land holdings, and estimated production by crops of subsistence regions. Livestock by species are to be counted, and estimates made of gross capital formation in agricultural machinery and equipment.

Together with the summaries reported for forestry and fishing, the findings will indicate for the first time in such details how much of Africa exists outside a money economy, and how much has emerged into commercial channels, using cash as the medium of exchange.

UNITED STATES ECONOMIC POLICY IN AFRICA [7]

American direct investment in Africa south of the Sahara has always been a minor part of U.S. overseas financial activity.

[6] From *United States Foreign Policy: Africa; A Study,* prepared at the request of the Senate Committee on Foreign Relations, by Northwestern University Program of African Studies. United States. Senate. Committee on Foreign Relations. 86th Congress, 1st session. Supt. of Docs. Washington 25, D.C. '59. p 41-3.

It has been estimated that, for the whole of Africa, this amounted in 1929 to $92.4 million (out of a total of all world areas of $7,527.7 million); in 1936 to $83.4 million (out of $6,690.5 million); in 1943, $104.2 million (the total being $7,861.6 million); and in 1950, $298.6 million (out of the global sum of $11,788 million). In 1954 U.S. investment in Africa rose to $568 million, and in 1955 to $657 million, more than a sixfold increase in less than a decade. During the earlier period, the African share of U.S. investment abroad remained at a little over 1 per cent, then almost doubled to 2.5 per cent from 1943 to 1950. To double a small share, however, does not produce a large one, so that both in absolute and relative terms U.S. investments in Africa have remained small.

The capital invested is distributed unevenly, both as regards activity and area. The processing and sale of petroleum products and manufacturing accounted for over one-half of the American world total; two-thirds of all foreign direct investment in Africa has gone into petroleum, and mining and smelting. Three-fourths of all American investment in Africa has been made in the Union of South Africa and Liberia. In the Union, U.S. direct investment in 1943 was $50 million (of a total for Africa of $104.2 million); in 1950 $140.1 million (out of an over-all amount in Africa of $289.6 million). According to Union government statistics, American portfolio investment amounted to a further $22.8 million, with other types of property owned by Americans bringing the total of American investment in South Africa to $86.6 million. As for Liberia, where before World War II the Firestone interests had the only significant U.S. holdings, increased sale and use of petroleum products, the discovery of rich iron ore deposits and the opening of Liberian registration to foreign shipping caused a sharp rise in American investments there; $380 million in 1957 as against $82 million in 1950 and $17.5 million in 1943. Liberia has thus passed the Union, where in 1957 American investment totaled $305 million.

The proportion of U.S. investments in these two independent countries stands in contrast to holdings in the dependent territories. In 1950, for example, American direct investment in the then British possessions of West Africa amounted to $10.5 million, which is to be compared to the £42 million ($117.6 million) of direct and portfolio United Kingdom investment for the same year. This also holds for British East and Central Africa, and in lesser proportion for the Union of South Africa, where British investment, following the general patterns whereby economic ties established between a dependency and its metropole are continued after self-government, is larger than that of the United States. Reports of annual South African company meetings are published in London as well as in South African newspapers.

U.S. investments in the dependencies of other overseas powers are minimal, both in terms of our total commitments in sub-Saharan Africa and in comparison to sums invested by the metropolitan countries. Thus, by 1954, U.S. private investment in all French Equatorial Africa amounted to only $1,297,142, though mining operations in the Gabon Republic by a consortium in which U.S. companies are participating will materially increase this sum. The success of a recent loan floated by the Belgian Congo in the American securities market may also presage larger portfolio holdings by U.S. investors.

In seeking to account for the small proportion of U.S. funds invested abroad going to Africa, we may first consider the proposition generally advanced that investors, when placing their money in foreign ventures look for high return and political stability. Both these conditions were met in Africa, certainly at the beginning of this decade and earlier. In 1950, for example, the rate of return on all American overseas investment before foreign income taxes was about 26 per cent. For Africa as a whole, investment brought a calculated return of about 30 per cent before foreign income taxes. As regards stability, political controls were firmly in the hands of the metropolitan governments.

This suggests that yet another, a third factor, enters. Specifically, this involves the relationship of foreign investment to freedom of political and economic decision. Until recent years, investment in colonial territories from countries outside the metropole was not encouraged. Only when it became self-evident that the economic needs for development were beyond the capacity of the metropolitan governments to finance, was there hospitality to investment from other sources.

A growing interest in investment possibilities in Africa has been shown by Canada, Sweden, Holland, Switzerland, and West Germany. In all cases, of course, the preconditions of adequate return and political stability must be satisfied. For development projects of the magnitude of the Volta scheme or the Inga Dam, investors await political developments. But with stability and return reasonably assured, it may be anticipated that nations having capital for export, of which the United States is the most prominent, will increasingly respond to the opportunities presented by investment in African enterprises, and figure more and more in financing enterprises in African states.

These considerations of colonial as against independent status hold for trade, though they affect imports more than exports. In 1957 the African share of our total exports was 3.4 per cent, while our imports from the continent, mainly primary materials, made up only 4.4 per cent of what we purchased overseas. This, of course, reflects the size of the American financial commitment in the continent, for more American business activity would be correlated with greater U.S. investment. As economic development raises African standards of living, however, African market potentials become greater, and this in turn makes for more commercial activity, in which U.S. products compete with those of other industrialized countries, with the metropole, past or present, holding the dominant position.

Nigeria exemplifies this. In 1958, imports from the United Kingdom totaled £72.7 million, an increase of over £6 million above 1957 figures. Imports from Japan came to £19.4 million, from Western Germany £12.2 million, from the United States £9.7 million, from the Netherlands £8.8 million, and from Norway and India some £6 million each. Exports to Commonwealth countries and to France dropped in value, but Western Germany increased its purchases by almost 100 per cent, and the Netherlands by 50 per cent. The United States also took more

Nigerian products, while Japan moved from purchases that were only nominal to a total of more than £1 million.

U.S. grants and loans must be included in any analysis of American economic commitments in Africa. Again, because of the nature of the colonial situation, these have been minimal, totaling just under $800 million to the end of fiscal year 1957. Aid in these categories has been given principally through the International Cooperation Administration and its predecessors, through the Export-Import Bank, and the newer Development Loan Fund. A certain amount of American support for European countries with overseas possessions has been channeled to Africa, as in the case of the French counterpart funds. The colonial powers, however, have showed preference for financing their African needs themselves, so that outside participation on the governmental level has not been sought. It has been calculated that of total U.S. grants from 1945 to 1956, Africa received 0.15 per cent; of loans, African countries received only 2.12 per cent, of which over two-thirds went to the Union and the Federation. It is reasonable to assume that with the increase in the number of independent African countries, U.S. governmental aid commitments will materially increase.

IV. WEST AFRICA AND THE WORLD

EDITOR'S INTRODUCTION

Africa is destined to play an increasingly important role on the world stage. However, if the West tries to understand Africa's actions merely in terms of their meaning in the East-West struggle, Africa's position will certainly be misunderstood. Most African countries want to stay wholly neutral, to avoid the expense of entanglement in the cold war, to concentrate on their own overwhelming problems.

Their difficulties appear to them to be as vital and as difficult of solution as East-West relations appear in America. In order to indicate the vehemence of Africans on this subject, the first selection reprints some of the resolutions passed at the All African People's Conference held in December 1958. The fact that the language is flamboyant should not hide the depth of the feeling. The remaining articles in this section explore the future role of Africa in the United Nations, Africa's attitudes to East and West, and finally the position the United States should take toward Africa. The book concludes with a series of recommendations about the posture we should adopt as we try to keep abreast of changes in Africa.

RESOLUTIONS OF THE ALL AFRICAN PEOPLE'S CONFERENCE [1]

More than three hundred delegates representing 200 million Africans in 28 countries met at Accra, Ghana, from December 5 to 13, 1958, at a non-governmental conference. The group set up a permanent All African People's Conference with a secretariat in Accra, and also passed resolutions on racialism and discrimination, on imperialism and colonialism, on tribalism, religious separatism and traditional institutions, and on frontiers,

[1] From the texts of the resolutions reprinted in *Current History*. *Current History*. 37:41-6. Jl. '59. Reprinted by permission.

boundaries and federations. The . . . texts of [certain] resolutions follow: . . .

Imperialism and Colonialism

1. Whereas the great bulk of the African continent has been carved out arbitrarily to the detriment of the indigenous African peoples by European imperialists, namely Britain, France, Belgium, Spain, Italy and Portugal;

2. Whereas, in this process of colonization, two groups of colonial territories have emerged, to wit:

(a) those territories where indigenous Africans are dominated by foreigners who have their seats of authority in foreign lands, for example, French West Africa, French Equatorial Africa, Nigeria, Sierra Leone, Gambia, Belgian Congo, Portuguese Guinea, Basutoland, Swaziland and Bechuanaland,

(b) those where indigenous Africans are dominated and oppressed by foreigners who have settled permanently in Africa and who regard the position of Africa under their sway as belonging more to them than to the African, e.g. Kenya, Union of South Africa, Algeria, Rhodesia, Angola and Mozambique;

3. Whereas world opinion unequivocally condemns oppression and subjugation of one race by another in whatever shape or form;

4. Whereas all African peoples everywhere strongly deplore the economic exploitation of African peoples by imperialist countries, thus reducing Africans to poverty in the midst of plenty;

5. Whereas all African peoples vehemently resent the militarization of Africans and the use of African soldiers in a nefarious global game against their brethren as in Algeria, Kenya, South Africa, Cameroons, Ivory Coast, Rhodesia, and in the Suez Canal invasion;

6. Whereas fundamental human rights, freedom of speech, freedom of association, freedom of movement, freedom of worship, freedom to live a full and abundant life as approved by the All

African People's Conference on December 13th, 1958, are denied to Africans through the activities of imperialists;

7. Whereas denial of the franchise to Africans on the basis of race or sex has been one of the principal instruments of colonial policy by imperialists and their agents, thus making it feasible for a few white settlers to lord it over millions of indigenous Africans as in the proposed Central African Federation, Kenya, Union of South Africa, Algeria, Angola, Mozambique, and the Cameroons;

8. Whereas imperialists are now coordinating their activities by forming military and economic pacts such as NATO, European Common Market, Free Trade Area, Organization for European Economic Cooperation, Common Organization in Sahara for the purpose of strengthening their imperialist activities in Africa and elsewhere;

Be it resolved, and it is hereby resolved:

1. That the All African People's Conference vehemently condemns colonialism and imperialism in whatever shape or form these evils are perpetuated;

2. That the political and economic exploitation of Africans by imperialist Europeans should cease forthwith;

3. That the use of African manpower in the nefarious game of power politics by imperialists should be a thing of the past;

4. That independent African states should pursue in their international policy principles which will expedite and accelerate the independence and sovereignty of all dependent and colonial African territories;

5. That fundamental human rights be extended to all men and women in Africa, and that the rights of indigenous Africans to the fullest use of their lands be respected and preserved;

6. That universal adult franchise be extended to all persons in Africa, regardless of race or sex;

7. That independent African states ensure that fundamental human rights and universal adult franchise are fully extended to everyone within their states, as an example to imperial nations who abuse and ignore the extension of those rights to Africans;

8. That a permanent secretariat of the All African People's Conference be set up to organize the All African Conference on a firm basis;

9. That a human rights committee of the Conference be formed to examine complaints of abuse of human rights in every part of Africa and to take appropriate steps to ensure the enjoyment of the rights by everyone;

10. That the All African People's Conference in Accra declares its full support to all fighters for freedom in Africa, to all those who resort to peaceful means of nonviolence and civil disobedience as well as to all those who are compelled to retaliate against violence to attain national independence and freedom for the people. Where such retaliation becomes necessary, the Conference condemns all legislation which considers those who fight for their independence and freedom as ordinary criminals. . . .

On Frontiers, Boundaries, and Federations

1. Whereas the great mass of African peoples are animated by a desire for unity;

Whereas the unity of Africa will be vital to the independence of its component units and essential to the security and general well-being of African peoples;

Whereas the existence of separate states in Africa is fraught with the dangers of exposure to imperialist intrigues and of resurgence of colonialism even after their attainment of independence, unless there is unity among them; and

Whereas the ultimate objective of African nations is a commonwealth of free African states;

Be it resolved, and it is hereby resolved by the All African People's Conference, that the Conference:

(a) endorses Pan Africanism and the desire for unity among African peoples;

(b) declares that its ultimate objective is the evolution of a commonwealth of free African states;

(c) calls upon the independent states of Africa to lead the peoples of Africa towards the attainment of this objective; and

(d) expresses the hope that the day will dawn when the first loyalty of African states will be to an African commonwealth.

2. Whereas, as a first step towards the attainment of the broad objective of an African commonwealth, the independent states of Africa should amalgamate themselves on the basis of geographical contiguity, economic interdependence, linguistic and cultural affinity;

Whereas linguistic, religious and cultural divisions and national sovereignty should be subordinated to the overriding demands of Pan African unity where common geographical and economic considerations and national interests suggest the grouping of certain states;

Whereas amalgamation, federation or groupings should only take place between independent states governed by Africans;

Whereas each state should decide to which group it wishes to adhere, by a referendum based on universal adult suffrage;

Whereas regional federations of groups should be regarded as a means to an end and should not be prejudicial to the ultimate objective of a Pan African commonwealth by hardening as separate entities and thereby impeding progress towards a continental commonwealth;

Whereas the people of North Africa have taken the initiative towards a North African federation, and there is a strong desire in West Africa for a West African grouping;

Whereas it is desirable that other groups should emerge in Africa, provided they are not federations visualized or constituted by colonial powers against the wishes of the African people, since such federations are a ready weapon in the hands of colonial governments and white settlers for the oppression of the African people; and

Whereas countries which do not appear to fall naturally into any geographical group should, after their attainment of independence, decide by democratic processes whether to adhere to existing groups or to evolve different groups;

Be it resolved, and it is hereby resolved by the All African People's Conference, that the Conference:

(a) endorses the desire in various parts of Africa for regional grouping of states;

(b) advocates that such groupings should be based on three principles, namely:

  (i) only independent states and countries governed by Africans should come together;

  (ii) the establishment of groups should not be prejudicial to the ultimate objective of a Pan African commonwealth;

  (iii) adherence to any group should be based on the wishes of the people ascertained by referendum on the basis of universal adult suffrage; and

(c) recommends that countries which do not appear to fall naturally within any group should decide by similar means whether to adhere to any group or to evolve different groups.

3. Whereas artificial barriers and frontiers drawn by imperialists to divide African peoples operate to the detriment of Africans, and should therefore be abolished or adjusted;

Whereas frontiers which cut across ethnic groups or divide peoples of the same stock are unnatural and are not conducive to peace or stability;

Whereas leaders of neighboring countries should cooperate towards a permanent solution of such problems which accords with the best interests of the people affected and enhances the prospects of realization of the ideal of a Pan African commonwealth of free states; . . .

Be it resolved, and it is hereby resolved by the All African People's Conference, that the Conference:

(a) denounces artificial frontiers drawn by imperialist powers to divide the peoples of Africa, particularly those which cut across ethnic groups and divide people of the same stock;

(b) calls for the abolition or adjustment of such frontiers at an early date;

(c) calls upon the independent states of Africa to support a permanent solution to this problem founded upon the true wishes of the people. . . .

On Establishment of a Permanent Organization

Whereas the imperialist powers of Great Britain, France, Spain, Portugal, Belgium, and the Union of South Africa have, between them, deprived various people of Africa of their freedom and liberty; and

Whereas the leaders of political parties and trade unions in Africa gathered in Accra between the fifth day of December 1958 and the thirteenth day of December 1958, are irrevocably resolved to wage a final assault upon the denial of freedom, liberty and fundamental human rights to people of Africa;

Be it resolved that the All African People's Conference be established with a permanent secretariat in Accra, with the following aims and objects:

(a) to promote understanding and unity among peoples of Africa;

(b) to accelerate the liberation of Africa from imperialism and colonialism;

(c) to mobilize world opinion against the denial of political rights and fundamental human rights to Africans;

(d) to develop the feeling of one community among the peoples of Africa with the object of the emergence of a United States of Africa;

And that the conference of the secretariat should be governed by the rules approved for that purpose at this Conference.

AN AFRICAN BLOC TAKES SHAPE IN THE UNITED NATIONS [2]

A fiery speech in the United Nations General Assembly by Sékou Touré, the President of Guinea, [has] dramatized the complex problems arising out of the awakening of Africa.

The struggle of the Asian peoples for independence, which was one of the most important developments of the first postwar decade, has ended with the virtual liquidation of the British, French and Dutch empires in Asia. A like development is under way in Africa, and the African UN members' assertion of their identity has gone so far as to weaken the Asian-African bloc in the Assembly.

As the head of Africa's newest state, which . . . [in 1958] rejected General de Gaulle's offer of autonomy within the French community and opted for independence, Mr. Touré demanded that France, Britain, Belgium, Portugal and Spain renounce all of their African possessions. Moreover, he was contemptuous of the African leaders who have settled for less than complete independence from the French.

All the new states that have been established or are being established south of the Sahara seem to share these feelings. To the north, Tunisia and Morocco take a more moderate position. But most of the nine African members of the United Nations are so vociferously anticolonial that wise statesmanship will be necessary to prevent the Soviet Union from turning this into an anti-Western attitude.

The United Nations already has twenty-nine members of the Asian-African group, not counting Nationalist China, Israel and the Union of South Africa, which are excluded from the bloc.

With the exception of such allies of the United States as Turkey, Pakistan, Japan, the Philippines and Thailand, practically all the group's members are neutralists. When these have joined with the nine Soviet bloc nations and with Sweden and other

[2] From "Now an African Bloc Takes Shape in the U.N." by Thomas J. Hamilton, New York *Times* correspondent. New York *Times News of the Week in Review.* p E3. N. 8, '59. Reprinted by permission.

European neutrals, they have made it impossible for the Western countries to muster the necessary two-thirds majority for important action in the eighty-two member General Assembly.

In the early days of the United Nations, when its membership was slowly rising to sixty, it was a different story. The twenty Latin-American countries, which follow the leadership of the United States on most issues, together with the allies of the United States in Western Europe, the British Commonwealth and Asia, assured a dependable majority.

The relative strength of the Western powers suffered a drastic reduction after Canada engineered the mass admission deal in 1955. If the Asian-African bloc were as solid now as it was then, the position of the Western powers, at least on colonial issues, would be hopeless.

In recent months, however, the African section of the Asian-African group has taken such an extreme anticolonial position that the Asians are beginning to draw back.

Friction has reached the point where the African delegates not only failed to show up at a recent meeting of the combined group but held a separate meeting of their own.

This started becoming evident . . . [in] February [1959] during an Assembly discussion of French plans to grant independence to the French Cameroons in 1960. The Africans argued that the provisional government of the Cameroons had been installed by France and would serve French interests if it were in power when independence was granted. They insisted that the United Nations hold new elections . . . [this year].

However, India and many Asian members felt that the previous elections had been fairly conducted, and the African view did not prevail. Some African delegates angrily asserted in the corridors that India had taken this position in the hope of protecting the interests of the Indian trading communities in Africa.

However this may be, two issues at the current sessions have accentuated the division. . . . [In October 1959] the Africans introduced a resolution threatening to hale the Union of South

Africa before the International Court of Justice to account for its administration of South-West Africa. . . .

The lack of Asian support compelled the Africans to be satisfied with a milder resolution.

Similarly, the more determined anticolonial Africans tried last month to induce the Asian-African group to sponsor a resolution "deploring" the French determination to hold a nuclear test explosion in the Sahara. The Asians, together with the more moderate Africans, preferred somewhat milder language, and their view prevailed. Of course, the Sahara issue did not directly concern the Asian nations. . . .

Whatever the reason, the division within the Asian-African group unquestionably exists. India, after having held the leadershop of the group throughout the history of the United Nations, is now being subjected to African reprisals. . . .

The significant fact is that the African brand of anticolonialism is considerably stronger than the Asian product, and that the admission of more African members will strengthen African influence in the United Nations.

ATTITUDES OF AFRICANS TOWARD EAST AND WEST [3]

One of the most widely distributed fables in sub-Saharan Africa tells how a small, clever creature—a rabbit, or spider, or antelope—becomes ruler of the beasts. He challenges first the elephant, then the rhinoceros to a tug of war, stipulating only that the rope be a long one. Setting the same time for the two contests, he causes the powerful animals, who cannot see the other end of the rope, to pull against each other. When neither can prevail, he comes forward to proclaim himself the winner over each.

Africans are a proverb-using people, and the fable is often the elaboration of a social value. This tale evokes for them a congenial answer to the question of their position in the East-West struggle. From a hardheaded African point of view, non-

[3] From *United States Foreign Policy: Africa; A Study,* prepared at the request of the Senate Committee on Foreign Relations, by Northwestern University Program of African Studies. United States. Senate. Committee on Foreign Relations. 86th Congress, 1st session. Supt. of Docs. Washington 25, D.C. '59. p 70-2.

alignment means noninterference in the quarrels of others. The African position on nonalignment has been explicitly stated many times; a few examples will make the point. "We have no part in the East-West conflict," wrote M. Alioune Diop, publisher of the influential journal *Présence Africaine.*

"We offer to everyone the hand of friendship. We neither take the East nor the West. We are going forward to produce a positive African personality," was the way Mr. Tom Mboya, president of the All African People's Conference, put it in his closing address. A "Draft Memorandum," prepared by Ghana in connection with the April 1958 Conference of African States, said:

> The time has come for Africa to view the international situation in the light of her own interests. Where it suits her long-term interest to ally herself with particular countries in Europe, the Western Hemisphere and Asia, she might come to specific arrangements to safeguard her interests.

At the present time, the concerns of Africans are so centered on attaining their objective of freedom from colonial controls that for them other issues are secondary. Alignment with East or West, that is, enters into the African position only to the extent to which it bears on the major question of the achievement and maintenance of self-government. As all who know at first hand the ordering of personal relations within African societies can testify, Africans have long been skilled in the strategy of bargaining with those who wield power. No better expression of this traditional approach as applied to the world scene could be had than in the assertion last April by M. Sékou Touré at the Conakry meeting of the Executive Committee of the All African People's Conference that "Africa will never become the vassal of any bloc, of any group, but she will of necessity have to take account of the external forces working in her behalf or to her detriment."

While the position taken by African leaders is essentially the traditionally congenial one of noncommitment, there is good evidence of an underlying pro-Western orientation. As we have observed, Africans are impressed with Russian scientific and technical achievement; but we find few indications of their acceptance of Communist ideology. The Sudan is reported to have banned attendance at the Communist-sponsored World Youth Festival held in Vienna . . . [in 1957] and the Government party in Ghana to have publicly expressed its disapproval of it. As we have said, Africans are keeping themselves informed of Chinese methods of mobilization and use of manpower in furthering economic development and the most effective use of natural resources; but they are also impressed with what Israel has accomplished along the same lines since she has become self-governing.

Ideological considerations aside, the Africans would prefer to deal with the countries of the West rather than those of the East, if only because they are more familiar with them and their ways. When Guinea, following her vote for independence, needed arms because of the withdrawal of all French equipment, she turned first to the United States. According to report, this was not done through customary diplomatic channels, and the request is said never to have reached the responsible American officials. Parenthetically, we might recall here that the United States has no official representation in Conakry, while the French had trained no Africans for the diplomatic service. Only after her overtures to the United States brought no reply did Guinea accept arms from Czechoslovakia. When the President of Guinea in Conakry was making the statement just quoted, his ambassador in Paris, M. Nabi Youlu, in emphasizing that Guinea had made no political choice between East and West, said: "Guinea has concluded economic agreements with the countries of the East, but no proposition for aid has been made by the countries of the West."

Relations of the West with Guinea have become less equivocal with the writing of monetary agreements with France, with the appointment of a U.S. ambassador to Conakry, with the continuation of mining and other activities by American, Canadian, and European interests. It is also well to bear in mind that Guinea, as the African independent country oriented farthest toward the left, is not typical. It is, rather, a test case. Elsewhere in Africa, in the independent countries and those moving toward independence, the United States, particularly, profits from the many years of scientific and educational work American agencies have carried on there, while our technological resources and financial position, the more taken for granted because they do not have the dramatic character of new developments, nonetheless set goals for African striving.

As every American with specialized knowledge of Africa has stressed, there is little question that though Soviet advance in Africa has thus far been negligible, the countries of the Communist bloc can be expected to take every opportunity to fish in troubled waters. For the United States, in its global concern with international alignments the importance of the position taken by independent African nations cannot be overstated. In this part of the world, the democracies retain the initiative; it is essential that they do not give it over into other than African hands. By their understanding and their acts they have it still largely in their power to determine the extent to which Africa will remain friendly to them, or drift toward the Soviet orbit.

AGAINST AMERICAN INFLUENCE [4]

When one has been entrusted with a share of the responsibility for the destiny of young African states and wants to help them play a full role in international life and transform themselves into modern countries, it is easy enough to see the difficulties which bar the way, in a world subject to the conditions of the cold war.

We have been able to avoid the turning inward which is sometimes characteristic of newborn nationalism, considering this to be out of date, and we have determined instead to open ourselves up to the world.

Just as many hopeful young men approach life in the conviction that it is governed by the highest principles, we had imagined that the great powers, burdened with the memory of a terrible war, would seek the paths of friendship and that their

[4] From "No American Influence in Africa" by Hammadoun Dicko, socialist representative for the Soudan in the French Parliament. *Western World.* 2:27-31. Ap. '59. Reprinted by permission.

solidarity, stimulated by the appearance of new peoples on the stage of history, would give a new aspect to international relations.

We are eager to make our full contribution to the world and to peace, in our turn. So that we may be able to discharge our responsibility fully, we ask those who wish to be our friends for their understanding and generosity and also for their respect for our freedom and our own special character.

I hope more than anything else that readers will see in these lines the testimony of a man, an African, passionately devoted to the defense of freedom and human dignity, who has actively taken part in the emancipation of his country. It is written by one who believes that American influence in Black Africa would constitute a danger, threatening not only to compromise the normal development of former colonial peoples but also the very future of the free world.

Before taking up the problem presented by the possibility of the extension of American influence to the African continent, it is necessary to recall for a moment the great adventure through which most of its peoples have passed in the past few years.

This adventure began right after the war with the collapse of European power.

Conscious of its indisputable superiority in every field, and driven by irresistible dynamics, Europe had extended its sway over vast areas of the world. In the course of centuries, and especially during the nineteenth century, Europe had annexed enormous territories, which were subject to its exclusive influence and in which no other power could seriously think of disputing its plans. On the eve of the last war, Europe cherished the idea of a comprehensive integration of the peoples living under its control and of the creation of a universal political entity.

To prepare for this development, it was essential to change the colonized people, first of all by depersonalizing them. We were encouraged to forget our history, our culture, to abandon our own institutions. To inculcate the idea of our new loyalty, school children in French West Africa and French Equatorial Africa, were henceforth taught that their ancestors had been Gauls—so necessary was it, even by such a fiction, to prove that everything came from Europe.

Helpless and resigned to having our own destiny escape us, knowing that our fate was eventually to become a faithful and impersonal image of the West, we watched the development of these grandiose plans.

The peoples of Africa were not prepared to see European power tottering, and it was reasonable to fear that they would sink into complete chaos. This terrible danger was avoided by what it is proper to call the "African miracle." The Negro peoples woke up; Africa rediscovered Africa, with its own vitality, history, traditions and culture, its own sense of humanity, its new faith in the future and above all its own inexhaustible springs of wisdom. All the things which had been mistrusted or misunderstood by the colonizers once more became real values and a basis for higher aspirations. It was to the credit of Europe that it understood this miracle. Here I think especially of France, which forthwith reconsidered its whole African policy and carried out a drastic modification offering us its help in getting through the first exciting but difficult years of our reborn freedom.

Confronted by this new phenomenon, the emancipation of colonial peoples, the first reactions of the United States were deeply appreciated in Africa. A great man personified America's generous attitude—Franklin D. Roosevelt. Because he believed that his country had a duty toward these awakening masses, his action was criticized as idealistic and impractical and the fact was disregarded that moral principles strengthen those who submit to them and often point the way to a better future. To help restore dignity to a people does not necessarily lead to disappointment, but usually to the contrary. I am convinced that if such a policy as Roosevelt's had been continued, the defense of the free world would have been better assured, for we should have felt more secure in our freedom, and should have better understood our future. We should have placed in the United States a confidence unmarred by the reserve which we are compelled to express today.

Was this too fragile a policy in the face of the threat posed by Communist penetration? In any case, solutions designed to have more immediate effectiveness were chosen.

Conscious of being the leading defender of the free world, the United States felt every gain made by the Communist bloc as a body blow. It was possessed with anxiety, especially in Asia, in considering the great vacuum left by Europe, and believed, right or wrong, that these underdeveloped countries were the zone of expansion dreamed of by the Communists. Henceforth, confronted by an urgent need to submit these countries to American influence, the moral obligations and noble motives which impelled Roosevelt were dissipated as the division of the world into two blocs appeared inevitable—no part of the world was to be left free of one or another of these influences.

For us, the former colonial peoples, whose destiny had long been a pawn for others, following a brief interlude of joy in our reborn freedom, this projected division of the world presented a new and immediate threat to our future. If American domination was to be extended over Africa, it would be no use to try to persuade us that this was done for our own protection and to save us from more evil alternatives. We are perfectly clear: we can see for ourselves what is going on at the international level—and it is easy enough at ths stage to identify the term *influence* with *exploitation*. . . .

Nevertheless, some underdeveloped countries have agreed voluntarily and sometimes rather hastily to place themselves under the influence of the United States. They were tempted by the substantial material aid offered to them by America, at the price of various political or strategic concessions. The bargain seemed honest and safe. But does it secure the future? Does it not—for reasons which it will some day be difficult to justify—alienate the cherished independence of the peoples and offer to future generations a future without pride—or more probably a future of revolt and ultimate adherence to the Communist camp, which neither America nor these peoples had desired in the beginning?

I do not believe that Africa in general will react in the same way as some of these countries have—not so much because it is inherently suspicious of all American initiatives but because it will first of all want to know the spirit in which these are put forward. This is an elementary reflex and a reasonable precaution for which no one can blame Africa. . . .

I shall not conceal the fact that America's way of giving is disturbing to us. Our concern is not based only upon abstract considerations but primarily upon pragmatic observations. Speaking of such observations, is it not shocking to see enormous sums handed out by the United States for the exclusive benefit of potentates, simply because they are willing to swear an oath of allegiance—just as if they could provide assurance that their peoples will not fall under Communist control? The debasement of these potentates having been achieved, it is sad to realize that their peoples are subject to another debasement, that which comes from misery and enslavement.

There is a more subtle danger, but one of the same character, which threatens the underdeveloped countries. We have already been able to note its effects in various parts of the world: Wherever America decides to extend its sphere of influence we see the Soviet Union reacting and setting its own security machinery into motion. A battle of influence is begun, marked by demagogic bidding and counter-bidding. . . .

It is healthy for America to be told again and again that in such battles of influence it does not have the winning cards. The U.S.S.R. which was an underdeveloped country itself until very recently, understands the aspirations of these peoples; it has perfected techniques of propaganda whose effectiveness needs no further demonstration; it asks nothing in exchange for its gifts, it does not chastise the recalcitrants, and it knows how to wait—all of which gives it a very clear advantage.

Africa does not refuse the friendship of America: Africa wants this friendship. What it does refuse is to live within the American orbit. Africa hopes with all its heart that the word *influence,* with all its ambiguity, will be abandoned in international relations, and that new and just means will be found to cement the unity of the free world. Otherwise, it will one day be easy for the Soviet Union to sharpen the nationalist feelings of young peoples and lead them toward a destiny which they have not chosen for themselves.

A UNITED STATES POLICY FOR THE NEW AFRICA [5]

In the political field, our most promising opportunity at the moment is to relax pressure on Africans to join the Western camp. Such clichés of the cold war as the "battle for men's minds" and the "uncommitted nations" have outlived their usefulness. The trouble with the slogan "battle for men's minds" is that it seems to imply that Africans must somehow lose their minds to either the Russian or the American mentality. And that is just what African leaders don't want to do. They want to be distinctively African. The phrase "uncommitted nations" is even more outmoded because Africans made it abundantly clear at the international conferences they held in 1958 that they *are committed* to the neutralist, or non-alignment, or non-involvement idea of a distinctively African personality making itself felt as a force in world affairs.

The most we can reasonably hope for is that Africa's new leaders will decide upon neutrality with a Western orientation. The current ferment of nationalist, Pan Africanist, and related ideas indicates that many Africans may become as sensitive to American or Russian pressure as they are to that of Western Europe. The most influential great power in the new Africa may therefore be the power that succeeds in making its influence and its presence felt in the most unobtrusive way.

On the controversial colonial question there is little room for dramatic and positive American action. Our basic support of the principle of self-determination is inevitably clouded by our ambiguous position in practice. The critics who blame Western defense interests for this ambiguity are only partly right. It is also the result of our growing realization that new colonial poli-

[5] From article by Vernon McKay, professor of African studies, School of Advanced International Studies, the Johns Hopkins University. *Current History*. 37:1-6. Jl. '59. Reprinted by permission.

cies since World War II have produced impressive political, economic and educational advances in preparing Africans for self-government. Fortunately our dilemma on colonial issues, caused by our need for friends in both Europe and Africa, is declining as colonies disappear. . . .

Expansion of Economic Aid

Our best opportunity in Africa lies in the economic and educational, rather than the political field. We can help both Africa and the United States by assisting the new and emerging states in building economic and educational foundations for political freedom. In doing so, we should bear in mind that the conditions essential for the really successful operation of democratic institutions are not likely to exist in most of Africa in the foreseeable future. We should continue to foster democratic ideals, best of all by strengthening American democracy, but we will undermine our own objectives if we succumb to cynicism when new states fall short of these ideals.

The most we can reasonably hope for in the new Africa is enough political stability to make possible, with foreign aid, the eventual attainment of a self-sustaining stage of economic growth. If the new states can attain this stage, it may then be possible for their peoples to have the freedom of choice necessary to strengthen their democratic ideals and parliamentary institutions. The most important single step we can take in Africa today, therefore, is to expand our economic aid and technical assistance program.

There is admittedly a contradiction in the above argument if it is true that the most influential great power in the new Africa may be the power whose influence and presence is the least obtrusive. We cannot expand American aid without making the American presence more obvious. This is simply another of the dilemmas we must learn to live with.

When the honeymoon of independence is over, the new states of Africa are certain to enter a period of economic disappointment and frustration. Since human beings everywhere look for scapegoats the vulnerability of the United States to emotional criticism is likely to mount in direct proportion to the expansion of the American presence. A good example is the anti-American rioting in Bolivia in March, 1959, which was partly motivated by "the feeling that too many North Americans are working here on programs that are not coming up to expectations."

Despite this danger, the risk involved in expanding our aid to Africa is smaller than the risk of doing little or nothing. Let us therefore accept the dilemma and concentrate on improving our methods of extending aid in such a way as to minimize the objectionable qualities of the American presence. Although there are no easy ways of minimizing our presence while expanding our program, three steps might help toward this end.

First of all we need to improve the training of the administrators and technicians in our aid projects in order to broaden and deepen their understanding of African areas and peoples. An African training program for United States officials in the International Cooperation Administration, now under consideration, could be of real value.

Secondly, we must combat our conscious and unconscious tendency to exaggerate the merits of American "know-how" and efficiency. In judging between what Africans want and what we think they need, we have a tendency toward a "Daddy knows best" attitude that is not far from the paternalism of the colonial relationship against which Africans are now rebelling. The more we are able to meet reasonable African requests, the more effective our policy is likely to be in the long run. This depends partly on the skill and tact of individual officers in attaining the happy medium, but it might also require a policy decision in Washington to give higher priority to psychological factors in aid projects of debatable economic value. The sharp eyes which our taxpayers and congressmen focus on ICA projects make this easier said than done. This is a good illustration of why Congress and the public must develop the right general attitude toward Africa. Our officials can't do it alone.

The third method that might help to minimize the American presence in Africa is a continually increasing degree of international cooperation in aid projects. A cooperative approach seems to me of cardinal importance. Not only are Africa's needs too great for us to meet alone, but cooperation has values of its own which should benefit all concerned. If we are closely linked with other nations in aid projects, moreover, we may run less risk of an ultimate African reaction against the United States.

A cooperative approach in aid projects could be undertaken in two directions. The first is to increase our contributions to the economic aid and technical assistance funds of the United Nations and its Specialized Agencies. Aid from the United Nations, as many observers have reiterated, is psychologically more palatable than aid from a single power because it lessens African feelings of dependency. Since Africa's needs are too urgent and extensive for the United Nations to satisfy, however, we might supplement United Nations efforts by exploring the possibility of new forms of multilateral cooperation. One possibility might be a regional economic organization or plan for Africa, initiated by Africa's independent states. They might, for example, invite the United States, India and the Western powers with African interests and experience to join them in creating an elastic multinational organization within which special bilateral and multilateral arrangements could be negotiated and coordinated. African states would participate on a basis of complete equality and might be donors as well as receivers of aid. In addition to channeling capital into Africa, a new multinational organization might operate some form of international civil service.

The grave shortage of administrative and professional personnel in the new Africa will make the recruitment of foreign technicians necessary for many years. What we need is a new method for transferring power to Africans on terms which make it mutually satisfactory for white administrative and technical personnel to continue in service until Africa has trained its own specialists. This requires a system that provides continuity of service, security and a multiracial *esprit de corps*.

An organization of this type might absorb the structure, personnel and functions of the eight-power Commission for

Technical Cooperation in Africa South of the Sahara and the related Foundation for Mutual Assistance, as well as the African work of the Overseas Territories Committee of the Organization for European Economic Cooperation. These organizations have done valuable work but are psychologically ill-adapted to the needs of the new Africa because they are considered an outgrowth of the age of colonialism.

If the creation of such a comprehensive organization proves impractical, fruitful cooperation on a smaller scale would be profitable. For example, in the emerging states of West Africa formerly under British rule, there are many opportunities for effective cooperation. An excellent illustration is the recent appointment of a nine-man team, including three Nigerian, three American and three British experts, to analyze the higher educational needs of Nigeria. This could be a pilot project of great importance. Nigeria and Ghana are not hostile toward the United Kingdom, and the British have a wealth of experience which we lack with the economic and educational development of Africa.

Educational Opportunities

In addition to the relaxation of political pressure and the expansion of economic aid through cooperative methods, an effective United States policy for the new Africa should place a high priority on the expansion of our educational exchange and assistance programs. Public and private educational exchange projects which bring Africans to the United States and send Americans to Africa are a broadening and deepening experience of immeasurable value. Even if economic aid backfires, the more Africans there are who know Americans as personal friends, the more difficult it will be to build up a stereotype of the United States as a money-grubbing giant with no appreciation of esthetic and spiritual values.

It is essential to win the confidence of African intellectuals, using the term in the broadest sense to cover leaders in all fields. It is they who set the patterns for Africans to follow.

It should not be forgotten that Communist strategy and tactics place a high priority on winning the student movements along with the intellectuals who set student fashions.

The fact that African leaders and students have suffered from racial discrimination in the United States is worrisome, but much has been done and can still be done through private efforts to improve this situation. Moreover, a recent study of the reaction of Africans to their treatment in the United States indicates that they generally reveal considerable sophistication. . . .

In addition to educational exchange programs there are outstanding opportunities in other forms of educational assistance. The International Cooperation Administration has made a grant to the Royal Technical College in Kenya, has helped to create a College of Agricultural and Mechanical Arts in Ethiopia, has sent survey teams to eastern Nigeria and to Tunisia to investigate the possibility of American aid in establishing new universities, and has fostered a number of other African educational projects. An increasingly important role in educational assistance is also being played by American private organizations, including missionary groups, business corporations, universities, and philanthropic foundations. Private agencies can do many things more effectively than governments.

The Main Challenge

The main challenge to United States policy in Africa is saliently summed up in important statements made recently by friendly chiefs of state in two of Africa's new countries. In the October, 1958, issue of *Foreign Affairs,* Prime Minister Nkrumah of Ghana wrote: "We have to modernize. Either we shall do so with the interest and support of the West or we shall be compelled to turn elsewhere. This is not a warning or a threat but a straight statement of political reality." In July, 1958, President Bourguiba of Tunisia said: "As long as our pro-Western policy bears fruit we shall not change it. Let us meet again in four or five years and compare the results" with those of "some of our Arab brothers in the East who think that their situation calls for assistance from Soviet Russia."

It would be hard to find plainer and more direct statements of the basic need for economic and educational aid to strengthen the policies of Africa's friendly leaders. The test of our quality as a nation lies in our capacity to carry such burdens with patience and forbearance.

RECOMMENDATIONS FOR FUTURE UNITED STATES POLICIES [6]

1. U.S. policy, in furthering its own best interests and in accord with the action of some of our NATO associates, should be guided by expectation of the primacy of Africans in all sub-Saharan Africa.

2. The United States must treat Africa as a major policy area, to be approached on a level of equality with other policy areas, particularly Europe, where African-American interests are involved. U.S. policy in Africa must be flexible, in view of the variations in the African Continent and the rapidity of the changes occurring there; imaginative in view of our traditional sympathy with the aspirations of peoples to direct their own affairs; and positive in shaping aid programs with a view to African needs rather than cold war instrumentalities.

3. U.S. policy in Africa must facilitate the implementation of mutual interests with African countries. It should favor their development free from outside interference, with governments that will live at peace with their neighbors and serve the best interests of their peoples, as these are defined in terms of thir own values, functioning so as to reduce racial tensions where these are a factor.

4. The United States should recognize that for African states a policy of nonalignment is in the best interests of the West and of Africa. On the assumption that most of sub-

[6] From *United States Foreign Policy: Africa; A Study,* prepared at the request of the Senate Committee on Foreign Relations, by Northwestern University Program of African Studies. United States. Senate. Committee on Foreign Relations. 86th Congress, 1st session. Supt. of Docs. Washington 25, D.C. '59. p 13-17.

Saharan Africa will soon be released from colonial controls, the United States must take the position that our strategic requirements there will be subsidiary to political considerations, and military aid secondary to technical assistance.

5. The United States should view with sympathy efforts to create wider associations of African states which will promote political and economic stability, and facilitate the extension of aid in the economic and technical fields.

6. The United States should extend to all African dependent territories the policy applied to Tanganyika, favoring the issuance of specific statements by the responsible authorities about when and how self-government is to be attained, since the more peaceful the transition to self-rule, the greater the likelihood that present orientations toward the West will be maintained by newly independent states.

7. The United States should exert its influence to assure peaceful resolution of conflict in the multiracial states of Africa. It should urge recognition of the interests of all concerned and the implementation of their rights, without regard to ethnic affiliation.

8. The United States must demonstrate that in Africa it applies its domestic policies aimed at achieving interracial good will and equality. Examples of this would be the extension to all government operations there of existing legislation forbidding dealings by government agencies with firms that practice racial discrimination; having U.S. missions apply nondiscriminatory rules in personnel policies as regards local staff; and requiring U.S. firms operating in Africa to show that they have used all legal means to comply with this principle in order to receive tax concessions.

9. The United States should greatly increase appropriations for African exchanges and educational programs of all kinds. Support should be given to projects that link American scholars and their counterparts in Africa, thereby making available to African countries our best educational resources. The number of fellowships for Africans to study in American institutions of higher learning and technology should be materially increased.

Existing programs to train specialists sent to Africa as technical experts or members of the Foreign Service, in the human aspects of their work, should be extended.

10. The United States, in order to play its role in providing technical aid for newly independent and emerging African countries, should facilitate steps to establish career services for technical assistance personnel on the international level in cooperation with other countries, through the United Nations and through its own governmental operations.

11. The United States should immediately reappraise its aid programs for sub-Saharan Africa in order to determine their adequacy in the light of the needs of the area and of American interests. To compound the effectiveness of future contributions, efforts should be made to develop regional arrangements, roughly analogous to the Colombo plan, that will provide a framework for cooperation among the countries of sub-Saharan Africa, the European Economic Community, the British Commonwealth, the United States, and other nations willing to participate in measures to promote economic growth in the area.

12. U.S. grants, loans, and technical assistance, whether given directly or through international agencies, should be channeled toward aiding countries of sub-Saharan Africa in building up an infrastructure of facilities in such fields as transportation, communications, health, and education, where local resources of capital and personnel are inadequate to permit these countries to implement these basic aspects of their developmental plans.

13. U.S. fund-granting agencies and international bodies on which the United States is represented should extend the range of their operations to provide for research into problems of soil management and the development of effective methods for growing, processing, and marketing crops. These matters should be included in the agenda of discussions and negotiations for loans or grants to the governments of African countries.

14. U.S. Government agencies, including the International Cooperation Administration, should be authorized and encouraged to initiate studies of how technical assistance and loan

or grant funds can best stimulate long-term economic growth and stability. In fulfillment of this objective, U.S. government agencies should make maximum use of the growing body of knowledge about African societies gathered by nongovernmental institutions.

15. To encourage American capital investment in that continent, the Department of Commerce should extend the series of economic studies of African countries treating of their commercial and industrial potentials. The United States should also extend the use of methods developed for guaranteeing private investments in newly independent African states, such as the International Cooperation Administration's investment guarantee program, which at the same time will promote the interests of these countries.

BIBLIOGRAPHY

An asterisk (*) preceding a reference indicates that the article or a part of it has been reprinted in this book.

BIBLIOGRAPHIES

World Affairs Center. Changing Africa and world affairs (prepared with the cooperation of the African-American Institute). The Center. First Avenue at 47th Street. New York 17. '59.

See also bibliographies of new literature in the various numbers of African Abstracts, Africa, *and* African Affairs.

BOOKS, PAMPHLETS, AND DOCUMENTS

Adam, T. R. Government and politics in Africa south of the Sahara. Random House. New York. '59.

Amamoo, J. G. New Ghana. Pan Books. 8 Headfort Pl. London. '58.

American Assembly. United States and Africa. The Assembly. Graduate School of Business. Columbia University. New York. '58.

American Universities Field Staff. Ghana: striking a balance between plus and minus. E. S. Munger. The Staff. 522 Fifth Ave. New York 36. '58.

Anderson, R. E. Liberia, America's African friend. North Carolina University Press. Chapel Hill. '52.

Bascom, W. R. and Herskovits, M. J. Continuity and change in African cultures. University of Chicago Press. Chicago. '59.

Bovill, E. M. Golden trade of the Moors. Oxford University Press. New York. '58.

Bowles, Chester. Africa's challenge to America. University of California Press. Berkeley. '57.

Buell, R. L. Liberia: A century of survival. University Museum. 33rd and Spruce Sts. Philadelphia 4. '47.

Burns, Sir Alan. History of Nigeria. Allen & Unwin. London. '48.

Carter, G. M. and Brown, W. O. eds. Transition in Africa: studies in political adaptation. Boston University Press. Boston. '58.

Church, R. J. H. West Africa; a study of the environment and of man's use of it. Longmans. New York. '57.

Cloete, Stuart. African giant: the story of a journey. Houghton. Boston. '55.

Cohen, Sir Andrew. British policy in changing Africa. Northwestern University Press. Evanston, Ill. '59.

Coleman, J. C. Nigeria: background to nationalism. University of California Press. Berkeley. '58.

Dean, V. M. Nature of the non-Western world. (Mentor Book) New American Library. New York. '57.

Fage, J. D. Ghana: A historical interpretation. University of Wisconsin Press. Madison. '59.

Foreign Policy Association. What goals for Africa's new leaders? (Fact sheet, Great Decisions, 1960) The Association. New York. '59.

*French Press and Information Services. Communauté, supplement to Number 150 of Documentation Française Illustrée. The Services. 972 Fifth Ave. New York 21. '59.

French Press and Information Services. Statement on the Community; address delivered before the French National Assembly, Paris, October 13, 1959. Michel Debré. The Services. 972 Fifth Ave. New York 21. '59.

Gardner, R. N. New directtions in U.S. foreign economic policy. (Headline Series no 133) Foreign Policy Association. New York. '59.

Geiger, Theodore. United States business performance abroad: TWA's services to Ethiopia. National Planning Association. 1606 New Hampshire Ave. N.W. Washington 9, D.C. '59.

Gunther, John. Inside Africa. Harper. New York. '55.

Hailey, M. H. 1st baron (Lord Hailey). African survey, revised 1956. Oxford University Press. New York. '57.

Hance, W. A. African economic development. Harper. New York. '58.

Haines, C. G. ed. Africa today. Johns Hopkins Press. Baltimore. '55.

Hatch, John. Everyman's Africa. Dennis Dobson. London. '59.

Hodgkin, Thomas. Nationalism in colonial Africa. New York University Press. New York. '57.

Huddleston, Trevor. Naught for your comfort. Doubleday. Garden City, N.Y. '56.

International Labor Office. African labour survey. (New Series no 48) The office. 917 15th St., N.W., Washington 5, D.C. '58.

Lystad, Robert. Ashanti: a proud people. Rutgers University Press. New Brunswick, N.J. '58.

Mead, Margaret, ed. Cultural patterns and technical change. (Mentor Book) New American Library. New York. '55.

*Munger, E. S. Liberia's economic and human progress; letter from Monrovia, October 5, 1958. American Universities Field Staff. 522 Fifth Ave. New York 36. '58.

Murden, F. D. Underdeveloped lands: revolution of rising expectations. (Headline Series no 119) Foreign Policy Association. New York. '56.

Murdoch, G. P. Africa: its peoples and their culture. McGraw. New York. '59.

Myrdal, Gunnar. Rich lands and poor: the road to world prosperity. Harper. New York. '57.

Nkrumah, Kwame. Ghana: the autobiography of Kwame Nkrumah. Nelson. New York. '57.

Sax, Karl. Population explosion. (Headline Series no 120) Foreign Policy Association. New York. '56.

Schiffers, Heinrich. Quest for Africa: two thousand years of exploration. Putnam. New York. '58.

Schweitzer, Albert. African notebook. Holt. New York. '39.

*Scott, John. Africa: world's last frontier. (Headline Series no 135) Foreign Policy Association. New York. '59.

Seligman, C. G. Races of Africa. Oxford University Press. New York. '57.

South African Institute of International Affairs. Africa south of the Sahara; an assessment of human and material resources. Oxford University Press. New York. '51.

Stapleton, G. B. Wealth of Nigeria. Oxford University Press. New York. '58.

Stephens, R. W. Population pressures in Africa south of the Sahara. (Population Research Project) George Washington University. Washington, D.C. '58.

Stillman, C. W. Africa in the modern world. University of Chicago Press. Chicago. '55.

Taylor, Chatfield. United States business performance abroad: the Firestone operations in Liberia. National Planning Association. 1606 New Hampshire Ave., N.W. Washington 9, D.C. '56.

Thompson, Virginia and Adloff, Richard. French West Africa. Stanford University Press. Stanford, Calif. '58.

United Nations. Economic and Social Council. Twenty-eighth session. Report of the first session of the Economic Commission for Africa. (Supplement no 10) International Documents Service. Columbia University Press. New York. '59.

United Nations. Secretariat. Department of Economic and Social Affairs. Economic developments in Africa 1956-1957. International Documents Service. Columbia University Press. New York. '58.

United Nations. Secretariat. Department of Economic and Social Affairs. Structure and growth of selected African economies. International Documents Service. Columbia University Press. New York. '58.

*United States. Senate. Committee on Foreign Relations. United States foreign policy: Africa; a study, prepared at the request of the Committee on Foreign Relations, by the Northwestern University Program of African Studies. 86th Congress, 1st session. Supt. of Docs. Washington 25, D.C. '59.

Reprinted in this book: p iv; p 13-17; p 27-9; p 35-9; p 41-3; p 70-2.

Ward, W. E. F. History of Ghana. Macmillan. New York. '59.

Wright, Richard. White man, listen! Doubleday. Garden City, N.Y. '57.

PERIODICALS

Africa. 6:20-1. Ja.-F. '59. U.S. policy on Africa. C. C. Diggs Jr.

Africa Special Report. 4:3-4. S. '59. Belgium tightens policy on Congo. Helen Kitchen.

Africa Special Report. 4:7. S. '59. A senator looks at Africa. H. H. Humphrey.

*Atlantic Monthly. 203:4+. Ap. '59. Atlantic report on the world today—Belgian Congo.

Atlantic Monthly. 203:29-33. Ap. '59. Emerging Africa. Barbara Ward.

Atlantic Monthly. 204:12+. S. '59. Atlantic report on Guinea.

Canadian Journal of Economics and Political Science. 24:152-65. My. '58. Ghana, the West, and the Soviet Union. D. C. Anglin.

Christian Science Monitor. p 9. F. 26, '59. Africa's future. W. A. Stringer.

Current Biography. 20:14-16. Ap. '59. Daniel A. Chapman.
Also: Current Biography, 1959. p 62-4.

Current Biography. 20:21-3. Je. '59. Tom Mboya.
Also: Current Biography, 1959. p 298-300.

Current Biography. 20:40-2. Je. '59. Sékou Touré.
Also: Current Biography, 1959. p 453-4.

Current Biography. 21:27-9. Ap. '60. Modibo Keita.

Current History. 34:65-74. F. '58. French rule in Africa. Keith Irvine.

*Current History. 34:91-8. F. '58. French West Africa. Carroll Quigley.

*Current History. 37:1-46. Jl. '59. New states of Africa.
Reprinted in this book: United States policy for the new Africa. Vernon McKay. p 1-6; Guinea outside the French Community. H. R. Rudin. p 13-16; Ghana: problems and progress. L. S. Kenworthy. p 17-22; Resolutions of the All African People's Conference, Accra, December 1958. p 41-6.

Economist. 189:sup 1-40. D. 13, '58. African revolution; the political economy of Africa South of the Sahara in the decade ahead.

Economist. 190:568-70. F. 14, '59. Afro-Asia's casting role.

Encounter. 12:3-13. My. '59. Trouble in the air: letter from Ghana. Peregrine Worsthorne.

Focus. 9:1-6. Ap. '59. Ghana. G. H. T. Kimble.

Foreign Affairs. 36:143-53. O. '57. Differing faces of Africa. Lord Hailey.

Foreign Affairs. 37:45-53. O. '58. African prospect. Kwame Nkrumah.

Foreign Policy Bulletin. 39:11-15. O. 1, '59. Africa's hours of decision. V. M. Dean.

*Foreign Policy Bulletin. 39:22-4. O. 15, '59. Is democracy possible in Africa? V. M. Dean.

*Fortune. 57:124-6+. Mr. '58. Africa joins the world. Curtis Prendergast.

History Today. 9:83-93. F. '59. Jacobins in Africa. Basil Davidson.

Holiday. 25:53-60+. Ap. '59. Portrait of a continent. Laurens van der Post.
Holiday. 25:62-3+. Ap. '59. Drums of history. John Gunther.
Holiday. 25:64-73. Ap. '59. Gallery of leaders.
Holiday. 25:74-5+. Ap. '59. The blacks. Peter Abrahams.
International Organization. 12:303-19. Summer '58. Economic development proposal for Africa: a new multilateral aid organization. Arnold Rivkin.
Isis. 49:62-72. Mr. '58. Civilized West looks at primitive Africa: 1400-1800; a study in ethnocentrism. Katherine George.
Journal of Geography. 58:180-6. Ap. '59. Economic change in Africa. W. A. Hance.
*Life. 46:100-10. Ja. 26, '59. Black Africa surges to independence. Robert Coughlan.
Life. 46:82-96. F. 2, '59. Stormy future for Africa. Robert Coughlan.
*Listener. 40:500-1. O. 2, '58. Three early African empires. Thomas Hodgkin.
Listener. 66:555-7. O. 1, '59. Whither West Africa. Ago Ogunsheye.
Look. 23:24-31+. Je. 23, '59. Inside Negro Africa. Ernest Dunbar.
National Geographic Magazine. 116:220-53. Ag. '59. Beyond the Bight of Benin. Jeannette Fiévet and Maurice Fiévet.
Negro History Bulletin. 22:60-1. D. '58. Some insight gained on new Africa. J. E. Allen.
New Commonwealth. 37:438-9. Jl. '59. What leadership from Nigeria? Kunla Akinsemoyin.
New Commonwealth. 37:440-2. Jl. '59. Ghana will soon be a republic.
New Commonwealth. 37:444-6. Jl. '59. Sierra Leone needs stability. N. A. Cox-George.
*New Commonwealth. 37:447-8. Jl. '59. Can the Gambia go forward alone? Michael Crowder.
New Republic. 140:9-11. Je. 15, '59. Guinea, balance wheel in West Africa?
New Statesman. 57:568+. Ap. 25 '59. Ideas for Africa. Basil Davidson.
New York Times. p 7. N. 2, '59. Asia-Africa bloc seeks GATT help. Robert Trumbull.
*New York Times. p 47. N. 2, '59. U.N. survey to banish much of Africa's mystery. Kathleen McLaughlin.
*New York Times. p E3. N. 8, '59. Now an African bloc takes shape in the U.N. T. J. Hamilton.
New York Times. p 9. N. 15, '59. Belgium reports on Ruanda crisis.
*New York Times. p 17. D. 13, '59. De Gaulle backs loose Africa ties. T. F. Brady.
*New York Times. p 20. Ja. 3, '60. Clashes spread over Cameroon. Homer Bigart.

*New York Times. p E4. Ja. 3, '60. Belgian Congo—a case history of nationalism in Africa. Homer Bigart.

*New York Times. p 1+. Ja. 4, '60. Gazetteer of emerging Africa: march to independence is swift. Milton Bracker.

*New York Times. p. 4. Ja. 25, '60. Crushing issues face Cameroon. Homer Bigart.

New York Times. p 10. Mr. 2, '60. Guinea cuts tie to French franc. Homer Bigart.

New York Times. p 6. Mr. 7, '60. Ghana gets plan to be a republic.

New York Times Magazine. p 48+. S. 14, '58. Africa, too, challenges us. Mason Sears.

*New York Times Magazine. p 8+. Je. 28, '59. Key questions for awakening Africa. Tom Mboya.

New York Times Magazine. p 10+. Jl. 12, '59. Africa: complex and uneasy continent. Milton Bracker.

*New York Times Magazine. p 24-30. N. 29, '59. Drums of change beat for Africa's tribes. Elspeth Huxley.

New York Times Magazine. p 19+. Mr. 27, '60. Africa needs time. J. K. Nyerere.

New Yorker. 35:114+. Ap. 18, '59. Our far-flung correspondents. Christopher Rand.

Newsweek. 52:48. O. 13, '58. Sékou Touré: glory at 40.

Political Quarterly. 30:131-40. Ap. '59. Nigeria's constitutional road to independence. Kalu Ezera.

Reporter. 16:31-4. My. 2, '57. Prison graduates take over Ghana. John Somerville.

Reporter. 18:25-7. Je. 26, '58. French Black Africa by-passes the tempest of nationalism. J. H. Huizinga.

SAIS [School of Advanced International Studies] Review. 3:9-15. Winter '59. Economic policy in emergent Africa. Bernard Blankenheimer.

Technical Assistance Newsletter [United Nations]. Issue No 50. Part II. F. '59. Technical assistance in Africa.

Time. 71:30. Ap. 28, '58. African personality: conference of Africa's independent nations.

Time. 73:24-30. F. 16, '59. Vive l'indépendance.

Time. 73:42. My. 11, '59. Vive.

Time. 73:30+. My. 18, '59. Old pro.

Time. 73:27. My. 25, '59. Sardauna.

Time. 75:22+. Mr. 7, '60. Kenya: ready or not.

*U.S. News & World Report. 46:92-7+. Ap. 20, '59. In the Congo's jungles, a boom and a ferment.

U.S. News & World Report. 47:22. Jl. 13, '59. People of the week.

*U.S. News & World Report. 47:72-8. Jl. 27, '59 Out of the jungles—new nations and problems

*United Nations Review. 5:5-10. F. '59. New era of economic cooperation opens in Africa.

United States. Department of State Bulletin. 40:524-9. Ap. 13, '59. Role of labor in African development; address delivered before the Eastern Labor Press Conference, New York, March 20, 1959. J. C. Satterthwaite.

United States. Department of State Bulletin. 40:744-9. My. 25, '59. United States and West Africa: a survey of relations; address delivered before the Institute of Foreign Affairs, Earlham College, Richmond, Virginia, May 1, 1959. J. C. Satterthwaite.

United States. Department of State Bulletin. 40:841-9. Je. 8, '59. Africa; our interests and operations; address delivered before the Institute on African Affairs, Mundelein College, Chicago, Ill., May 15, 1959. J. K. Penfield.

Vital Speeches of the Day. 24:110-13. D. 1, '57. French attitudes toward American problems. I. R. Fraser.

*Western World. 2:27-31. Ap. '59. No American influence in Africa. Hammadoun Dicko.

Western World. 2:32-5. Ap. '59 Africa cannot do without the United States. Rayford Logan.

Western World. 2:13-17. Ag. '59. Dark Africa at stake. André Blanchet.

World Today. 15:147-56. Ap. '59. Nationalism in Africa: the two Accra conferences.